OFFICE FOR DISARMAMENT AFFAIRS

Disarmament Study Series, No. 36

The Global Reported Arms Trade

Transparency in Armaments through the United Nations Register of Conventional Arms

A Guide to Assist National Points of Contact in Submitting Their National Reports

United Nations

New York, 2017

GUIDE TO THE USER

This special edition of the Disarmament Study Series is issued in implementation of the United Nations Disarmament Information Programme. It serves as a valuable addition to the reference section of public and university libraries, permanent missions, research institutes and specialized non-governmental organizations.

For the electronic version of all material contained in the Study Series, see https://www.un.org/disarmament/publications/studyseries/.

Symbols of United Nations documents are composed of capital letters combined with figures. Mention of such a symbol indicates a reference to a United Nations document.

UNITED NATIONS PUBLICATION
Sales No. E.18.IX.2
ISBN: 978-92-1-142325-9
eISBN: 978-92-1-362900-0
Print ISSN: 1014-2177
Online ISSN: 2412-0014

Contents

Preface

On the occasion of the twenty-fifth anniversary of the United Nations Register of Conventional Arms (UNROCA), the United Nations Office for Disarmament Affairs is pleased to consider the Register's implementation and continuing operation in this special edition of the Disarmament Study Series.

The present text is broader in scope than past Study Series editions, which have served solely as a compilation of reports on disarmament and non-proliferations issues by Groups of Governmental Experts. This volume, by contrast, includes a newly written overview of UNROCA for reference by Governments and the interested public, as well as original material to guide national points of contact in preparing and submitting reports for the Register. This new content comprises part 1 of the publication. Part 2 contains the report of the 2016 Group of Governmental Experts on the continuing operation of UNROCA and part 3 presents the text of the General Assembly resolution that established the Group.

Introduction

Why report arms transfers to the United Nations?

Governments have committed to report to the United Nations on their arms imports and exports. Sharing such information can create trust between countries, and it may help determine whether excessive or destabilizing accumulations of arms are taking place. It may also contribute to early warning and preventive diplomacy.

Transparency is as important for countries that are large-scale arms traders as it is for those importing or exporting few or no weapons.

In 1991, the General Assembly created the United Nations Register of Conventional Arms (UNROCA or "the Register"), an annual reporting mechanism through which Governments can share information on arms transfers they were involved in during the previous year.[1]

In its resolution establishing UNROCA, the General Assembly stated its determination to prevent the excessive and destabilizing accumulation of arms in order to promote stability and strengthen international peace and security, taking into account the legitimate security needs of States and the principle of undiminished security at the lowest possible level of armaments.

In short, if States behave in a predictable and transparent way, including through an open approach to arms transfers, they can build mutual confidence and help prevent conflict.

What do Governments report?

UNROCA has a two-tier system of reporting: one tier for transfers in seven pre-defined categories of heavy weapons, as well as small arms ("7+1"), and a second tier for additional background information.

Under the latter tier, States can report to UNROCA on their current holdings of weaponry, their procurement through national arms production and their relevant legislation and policies.

Why these particular weapons categories?

The ability of UNROCA to achieve its declared aims depends on its coverage of relevant weapons categories and the extent of participation by Governments. The Register focuses primarily on seven categories of major conventional weapons, and countries report the vast majority of transfers involving these weapons. After Member States established an option in 2003 to also report to UNROCA on transfers of small arms and light weapons, most countries that submit reports have included these additional armaments in their submissions.

A triennial review process

When the General Assembly created UNROCA, it called for regular reviews where participants would consider expanding the Register to include additional weapons systems. A

---

[1] United Nations General Assembly resolution 46/36 L, 9 December 1991.

Group of Governmental Experts has therefore reviewed UNROCA every three years, resulting in a number of modest expansions to its scope.

Participation

In its 25 years of operation, 170 Member States have submitted a report to UNROCA at least once, and most major exporters and importers of conventional arms have reported to the Register on a fairly consistent basis. The United Nations estimates that Governments report well over 90 per cent of international transfers in the seven categories of conventional arms.

UNROCA serves as a point of reference and inspiration for regional and international confidence-building mechanisms, as well as for arms control and transfer control instruments. The instrument is a central reference in the Arms Trade Treaty (ATT), as the scope of this Treaty virtually mirrors that of the Register.[2] Like UNROCA, the ATT obliges its States Parties to report annually on their transfers of weapons.

A tool for confidence-building

In its initial resolution, the General Assembly requested the Secretary-General to make available data on arms transfers for consultation by Member States at their request. Governments are thus encouraged to make use of the wealth of data reported to UNROCA.

> *... the General Assembly stated its determination to prevent the excessive and destabilizing accumulation of arms ... and the principle of undiminished security at the lowest possible level of armaments*

Transparency in armaments is not a goal in itself; annual reporting should be a building block for confidence-building actions. Submissions to UNROCA could, in particular, form the basis for regular bilateral or regional dialogue on defence plans, needs and cooperation.

The value of UNROCA to the Security Council

UNROCA is a tool for conflict prevention, but it is also relevant in conflict and post-conflict settings. In recent years, experts on monitoring panels of the Security Council sanctions committees have consulted the Register for data on arms transfers with a view to examining States' compliance with arms embargoes mandated by the Council.[3]

In particular, UNROCA has applications for security sector reform and peacebuilding in post-conflict situations, where there is often limited data on the quantities of weapons in circulation or even under government control. Such scarcity of data can increase the challenge of addressing questions of rearmament, which demand careful consideration when the time arrives to rebuild armed forces and law enforcement. Information provided to UNROCA, however, can form a basis for discussions regarding the need for military hardware in a State that has recently

---

[2] See, for example, ATT article 2.1 and article 13.3.
[3] See, for example, reported transfers to Yemen in S/2016/73, pp. 74-77.

emerged from conflict or come under review for potential elimination of an arms embargo. Notably, however, such recommendations do not address the assistance that is often necessary to properly execute such a country-wide baseline assessment of military holdings.[4]

Role of the United Nations Secretariat

The United Nations Office for Disarmament Affairs facilitates submission of national reports and makes all information received available on the United Nations website (www.un.org/disarmament/register).

The Secretariat also takes the following steps to enhance awareness of UNROCA:

- Circulating notes verbales to all Member States at the beginning of the year;
- Sending letters to regional organizations;
- Sending reminders to permanent missions in New York and to national points of contact;
- Encouraging timely submission of reports;
- Providing briefings to Member States and to disarmament fellows;
- Providing a user-friendly web platform and web-based reporting;
- Assisting States with technical queries;
- Developing online training modules;
- Updating and circulating information about national points of contact;
- Highlighting UNROCA both within and outside the United Nations system; and
- Presenting at workshops and other events.

Review and access to data

The procedures for UNROCA were developed by a Panel of Experts appointed by the Secretary-General in 1992. Periodic reviews of the operation of the Register and its further development have been conducted by Groups of Governmental Experts in 1994, 1997, 2000, 2003, 2006, 2009, 2013 and 2016.

The United Nations captures submissions to UNROCA in a multi-year online database. This ensures universal, user-friendly access to the full body of reported arms import and export information, fulfilling the essential promise of the United Nations Register of Conventional Arms of "transparency in armaments".

www.un.org/disarmament/register | Contact: conventionalarms-unoda@un.org

---

[4] The United Nations Secretariat stands ready to provide such assistance. Contact conventionalarms-unoda@un.org.

Part 1

Definitions and reporting practice

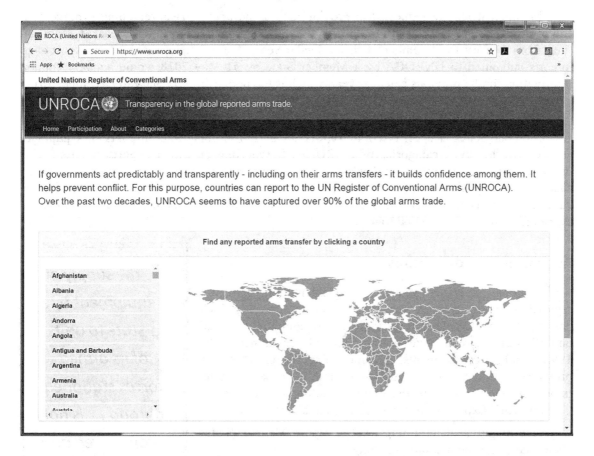

How UNROCA works

Annually, Member States are requested to provide data on the number of items in **seven categories, plus one (small arms)** that they imported into or exported from their territory.

Additionally, Member States are invited to provide **background information** regarding their **military holdings** and their **procurement through national production**. Furthermore, Member States are encouraged to inform the Secretary-General of their national **arms import and export policies**—for instance, when these policies have been updated—as well as **legislation and administrative procedures** on both authorization of arms transfers and prevention of illicit transfers.

Frequently asked questions

1. Are States requested to report all types of arms transfers, including orders and deliveries?

UNROCA is intended to only include data on the items in the specified categories of equipment imported into or exported from the territory of States in the previous calendar year. States are to report only those transfers that they consider to have occurred during the reporting year (i.e., actual transfers), in conformity with their respective national criteria for determining when a transfer takes effect. Transfers of decommissioned arms (e.g., for museums or film shootings) should not be reported.

2. What is the meaning of "calendar year"?

Member States are requested to provide data on an annual basis regarding exports from and/or imports into their territory during the calendar year prior to the year of reporting (i.e., from January to December of that calendar year). For example, the data on exports and imports submitted to UNROCA by a Member State by 31 May 2018 would actually contain information for the previous calendar year, which is the period from January to December 2017.

3. What if data on actual transfers of weapons are not available?

Member States **are expected to report on actual exports and imports** of equipment covered by the seven categories of UNROCA. If reporting on actual exports/imports is not possible, they may report on *authorizations* of exports and imports of conventional arms. In such cases, they should indicate in their national reports that the submitted data refer to authorizations. These should be seen as exceptional cases, and Member States should make every effort to report on actual transfers.[1]

Arms transfers: definitions

National practices regarding implementation of rules, regulations and procedures for exports and imports vary from country to country. Therefore, there is no commonly agreed definition of what constitutes an international arms transfer. The 1992 Panel of Governmental Technical Experts on UNROCA provided some guidance on what constitutes an export or an import for the purposes of the Register. Subsequent Groups of Governmental Experts have since reaffirmed this guidance.[2]

Accordingly, in determining what to report, Member States should take into account the following:

(a) International arms transfers involve, in addition to the physical movement of equipment into or from national territory, the transfer of title to the equipment and the transfer of control over the equipment.

> *... the supply of equipment by a State to units of its armed forces stationed abroad ... is not considered an international transfer.*

(b) An international arms transfer may occur without the movement of equipment across State borders if a State, or its agent, is granted title and control over equipment in the territory of the supplier State. Therefore, a transfer of arms to a State would occur when its forces stationed

---

[1] See Continuing operation of the United Nations Register of Conventional Arms and its further development. Report of the 2016 Group of Governmental Experts (A/71/259), para. 71.

[2] See "General and Complete Disarmament: Transparency in Armaments—Report on the Register of Conventional Arms—Report of the Secretary-General" (A/47/342), paras. 9-13.

abroad are granted title and control of equipment by the host country or any third State, or when the host country or any third State receives the title and control of such equipment. Additionally, an international transfer occurs if the owner of equipment temporarily stored or pre-positioned on the territory of another State grants the title and control of that equipment to the host country.

(c) If a State supplies equipment to units of its armed forces stationed abroad, it is not considered an international transfer because no transfer of national title and control takes place. Likewise, a State can temporarily store or pre-position equipment in the territory of another State with no transfer of title and control, and it is not considered an international arms transfer.

(d) Only transfers between United Nations Member States should be reported to UNROCA.[3]

Frequently asked questions

1. Can a transfer of arms occur without the physical movement of equipment across State borders?

Yes, a transfer of arms could occur either when title and control of equipment belonging to State A positioned overseas is transferred to the host State B, or when title and control over equipment is transferred to another State (State C) but the equipment remains on the territory of host State B. For instance, consider State A stationing a quantity of battle tanks (Category I) with a battalion in State B. When its mission concludes, State A agrees to sell the tanks to State B. When State B assumes the title and control of the tanks, both States would report this transaction as a transfer covered by UNROCA. The same reporting rule could apply if State A initially stores the tanks in State B rather than stationing them with an active military force as described above.

2. Must all equipment covered by UNROCA, which moves across international borders be reported?

No. As in the above example, if State A ships 20 of its own tanks to fortify its forces stationed abroad, its action is not considered an export (or import) because the shipment does not involve transfer of title or control of the equipment. Similarly, if State A ships these tanks to State B for the purpose of pre-positioning and they remain under the control of State A, neither State should report them as an export or import. Additionally, reports should not include decommissioned weaponry (e.g., for museums or film shootings).

3. How is the date of export or import determined?

Each State will determine this date based on its national criteria for determining the time when a transfer becomes effective. States are invited to indicate such national criteria when submitting their export and import data to UNROCA. However, the precise date of the transfer does not have to be reported; only the calendar year in question needs to be reported.

4. What if items covered by the Register are shipped from State A in 2015 but do not arrive at their destination in State B until 2016? In which year are they to be reported?

If the exporting State A maintains title and control over the equipment until it arrives in State B, both States A and B should report the transfer as occurring in the year 2016. However, if transfer of title and control take place in 2015 and the equipment remains in the territory of State A until 2016, the States should report the transfer as occurring in 2015.

---

[3] This is following a recommendation by the 2006 Group of Governmental Experts. See A/61/261, para. 126 (a).

Categories of equipment: 7+1

Annually, Member States are requested to supply data to UNROCA on their international transfers of the previous calendar year in the following seven categories of weapons:[4]

Category I   Battle tanks
Tracked or wheeled self-propelled armoured fighting vehicles with high cross-country mobility and a high level of self-protection, weighing at least 16.5 metric tons unladen weight, with a high muzzle velocity direct fire main gun of at least 75 millimetres calibre.

Category II   Armoured combat vehicles
Tracked, semi-tracked or wheeled self-propelled vehicles, with armoured protection and cross-country capability, either: (a) designed and equipped to transport a squad of four or more infantrymen, or (b) armed with an integral or organic weapon of at least 12.5 millimetres calibre or a missile launcher.

Category III   Large-calibre artillery systems
Guns, howitzers, artillery pieces, combining the characteristics of a gun or a howitzer, mortars or multiple-launch rocket systems, capable of engaging surface targets by delivering primarily indirect fire, with a calibre of 75 millimetres and above.

Category IV   Combat aircraft and unmanned combat aerial vehicles (UCAV)
Includes fixed-wing or variable-geometry wing aerial vehicles as defined below:

(a)   Manned fixed-wing or variable-geometry wing aircraft, designed, equipped or modified to engage targets by employing guided missiles, unguided rockets, bombs, guns, cannons or other weapons of destruction, including versions of these aircraft that perform specialized electronic warfare, suppression of air defence or reconnaissance missions.

(b)   Unmanned fixed-wing or variable-geometry wing aircraft, designed, equipped or modified to engage targets by employing guided missiles, unguided rockets, bombs, guns, cannons or other weapons of destruction.

The terms "combat aircraft" and "unmanned combat aerial vehicles (UCAV)" do not include primary trainer aircraft, unless designed, equipped or modified as described above.

Category V   Attack helicopters
Rotary-wing aircraft designed, equipped or modified to engage targets by employing guided or unguided anti-armour, air-to-surface, air-to-subsurface or air-to-air weapons and equipped with an integrated fire control and aiming system for these weapons, including versions of these aircraft that perform specialized reconnaissance or electronic warfare missions.

---

[4] The scope of UNROCA was defined by the General Assembly in its resolution 46/36 L of 9 December 1991 (annex, para. 2 (a)) and has been subject to periodic review by groups of governmental experts, which in some instances resulted in amendments to the descriptions of the categories. The present descriptions of the seven categories reflect an amendment to the heading and description of category IV, as recommended by the 2016 Group of Governmental Experts, which would enable UNROCA to capture data on international transfers of unmanned combat aerial vehicles. See page 51 (A/71/259, annex I).

Category VI   Warships
Vessels or submarines armed and equipped for military use with a standard displacement of 500 metric tons or above, and those with a standard displacement of less than 500 metric tons, equipped for launching missiles with a range of at least 25 kilometres or torpedoes with similar range.

Category VII   Missiles/missile launchers
(a)   Guided or unguided rockets, ballistic or cruise missiles capable of delivering a warhead or weapon of destruction to a range of at least 25 kilometres, and means designed or modified specifically for launching such missiles or rockets, if not covered by categories I through VI. For the purpose of the Register, this subcategory includes remotely piloted vehicles with the characteristics for missiles as defined above but does not include ground-to-air missiles.

(b)   Man-portable air defence systems (MANPADS).

In line with the "7+1 formula" adopted in 2016, States should report international transfers of **small arms and light weapons** (SALW) in parallel with the seven categories of UNROCA, using the separate standardized reporting form for SALW.[5]

UNROCA does not provide a definition of SALW. The standardized forms for reporting imports and exports of SALW include a list of small arms (revolvers and self-loading pistols, rifles and carbines, sub-machine guns, assault rifles and light machine guns) and a list of light weapons (heavy machine guns, hand-held under-barrel and mounted grenade launchers, portable anti-tank guns, portable anti-tank missile launchers and rocket systems, recoilless rifles and mortars of calibres less than 75 mm).

The form also allows for a State to report international transfers of other types of SALW under the lines labelled "Other".

Frequently asked questions

1.   Can a national report disregard certain categories?

Although the Register is a voluntary instrument, Member States reporting to UNROCA are expected to report on all categories.

2.   Do States have to report the transfer of SALW?

A large number of Member States have called for SALW to be included as an eighth category of UNROCA, and their adoption of the "7+1 formula" in 2016 lifted reporting of such transfers from additional background information to the level of the seven main categories.

---

[5] The 2016 Group reported as follows: "Taking into account calls to include small arms and light weapons as a new category in the Register, and at the same time considering the implications of such a step for the existing structure of the Register, the Group discussed the possibility of utilizing the seven plus one formula for a trial period to inform the deliberations of the next Group of Governmental Experts on the possible establishment of a new category for small arms and light weapons in the Register. The Group viewed the seven plus one formula as the reporting of international transfers of small arms and light weapons by Member States in parallel with the seven categories of the Register, using the standardized reporting form for international transfers of small arms and light weapons. Small arms and light weapons would not be represented as an eighth category on the standardized reporting form used for the seven existing categories. The Group recognized that such a trial use of the seven plus one formula, as well as the results of the proposed questionnaire, could greatly benefit the deliberations of the next Group of Governmental Experts on the possible inclusion in the Register of a new category for reporting small arms and light weapons." See page 46 (A/71/259, para. 75).

Therefore, reporting on SALW is expected to be done in parallel with reporting on the other categories of UNROCA. The 2019 Group of Governmental Experts will revisit the use of a "7+1 formula" in its deliberations on the possible establishment of a new category.

3.   Do States have to report the transfer of trainer aircraft?

Yes, they should report trainer aircraft that are "designed, equipped or modified to engage targets by employing guided missiles, unguided rockets, bombs, guns, cannons, or other weapons of destruction". Primary trainers with none of the above characteristics should not be reported.

4.   How do States determine which transfers of missiles and missile launchers to report under Category VII (a)?

If a missile launcher is an integral component of an item of equipment reported in Categories I to VI, there is no need to report it separately in Category VII (a) under "missiles and missile launchers". Only stand-alone (fixed or mobile) missile launchers are reported separately in Category VII (a). Missiles, however, are always reported in Category VII (a), regardless of the category of the equipment that launches them. For example, if State A imports 10 NEPTUNE missiles for use by warships, 5 for use by stand-alone missile launchers and 5 for use by combat aircraft, then all 20 missiles are still reported in Category VII (a).

5.   Category VII (b) includes man-portable air defence systems (MANPADS). What should be reported under this subcategory?

For reporting purposes, MANPADS are broadly defined as surface-to-air missile systems designed to be man-portable (i.e., carried and fired by a single individual). They also include other surface-to-air missile systems that are designed to be transported, operated and fired by more than one person (i.e., by a crew). MANPADS should be reported if the MANPAD system is supplied as a complete unit, as when a missile and launcher/grip stock form an integral unit. In addition, individual launching mechanisms or grip stocks should also be reported. Individual missiles not supplied with a launching mechanism or grip stock need not be reported.

6.   Under which category would a State report the transfer of one 210-mm multiple-launch rocket system (MLRS) with 30 rockets that have a range of 30 kilometres?

The MLRS falls within Category III, "large-calibre artillery systems". However, the rockets should be reported in Category VII under "missiles and missile launchers" if they have a range of at least 25 kilometres. (See also explanatory noted in the standardized reporting form.)

7.   Does UNROCA provide data on how many separate missiles and missile launchers are imported or exported by a specific country?

The number listed in Category VII normally indicates the total number of missiles and missile launchers combined. Therefore, it is not possible, using the data in UNROCA alone, to determine their separate numbers unless the State reported the data in a disaggregated manner or provided sufficient clarification in the optional "Remarks" column of the standardized reporting forms. With respect to MANPADS, which are accorded a unique status under UNROCA, a State may indicate the number of launching mechanisms or grip stocks if the items are supplied and reported as separate units.

Example

State F has exported to State K six FLYER missile launchers and 500 CATCH-22 missiles in 2015. The FLYER is a fixed ground-based launcher. The CATCH-22 is a surface-to-surface missile (SSM) with a conventional warhead and a range of 180 kilometres. The examples that follow illustrate how State F might report that export with different levels of transparency.

Version 1

State F has aggregated the missile launchers and missiles, and reports 506 items. This version meets the reporting requirement of the Register.

EXPORTS
Reports of international arms transfers
(According to United Nations General Assembly resolution 46/36 L)
Reporting country: F
Calendar year: 2015

A	B	C	D	E	REMARKS	
Category (I-VII)	Final importer State(s)	Number of items	State of origin if not exporter	Intermediate location (if any)	Description of item	Comments on the transfer
VII. (a) Missiles and missile launchers	K	506				

Version 2

In this version, State F has chosen to offer additional data, indicating in column C that the items are broken down into 6 missile launchers and 500 missiles. State F has used the "Remarks" column to identify the type of both the launcher and missile.

EXPORTS
Reports of international arms transfers
(According to United Nations General Assembly resolution 46/36 L)
Reporting country: F
Calendar year: 2015

A	B	C	D	E	REMARKS	
Category (I-VII)	Final importer State(s)	Number of items	State of origin if not exporter	Intermediate location (if any)	Description of item	Comments on the transfer
VII. (a) Missiles and missile launchers	1) K 2) K	6 500				1) Launcher, FLYER 2) Missile, CATCH 22	

8.   How do the reporting requirements apply to missile launchers on warships? Many ships covered by UNROCA have the capability to carry missile launchers. If a State exports a warship, should it report a missile launcher mounted on the ship as a separate transfer under Category VII?

No, missile launchers mounted on warships covered by UNROCA are considered to be integral components of the warship itself, and therefore, States should not report them as separate transfers of Category VII equipment. However, in reporting on transfers of warships, States have the option to clarify this point by indicating in the "Remarks" column of the standardized form if any and how many missile launchers are mounted on the reported warship(s).

If, however, a State exports or imports ship-based missile launchers separately from the ship (as is often the case in order to upgrade or modernize ships that are already in the inventory of a navy), these launchers would not be considered an integral part of the ship. Consequently, such missile launchers should be reported under Category VII of the Register.

9.   Should a State report the transfer of a fast-attack craft with a standard displacement of less than 500 metric tons equipped with missile launchers with a capability of delivering a missile beyond 25 kilometres? Should the launchers be reported under the Category VII (missiles and missile launchers)?

Although the craft has a standard displacement below the threshold for reporting (500 metric tons), its transfer should be reported because the craft is equipped for launching missiles with a range of at least 25 kilometres. The attack craft should be reported under Category VI (warships); the launchers need not be reported.

Example

In 2015, State B exported to State J two Hermes-class fast attack craft of 400 metric tons displacement. The ships are equipped with two twin missile launchers capable of delivering missiles to a range of 35 kilometres. The missiles for the ship were supplied prior to 2015.

EXPORTS

Reports of international arms transfers
(According to United Nations General Assembly resolution 46/36 L)
Reporting country: B
Calendar year: 2015

A	B	C	D	E	REMARKS	
Category (I-VII)	Final importer State(s)	Number of items	State of origin if not exporter	Intermediate location (if any)	Description of item	Comments on the transfer
VI. Warships	J	2			Hermes Class, 400-ton fast attack craft. See Note 1.	

Note 1: The ships are equipped with two twin missile launchers with a range of at least 25 kilometres.

10.   In the definition of Category VII (missiles and missile launchers), "ground-to-air missiles" are excluded and are not required to be reported. Does this mean that surface-to-air missiles mounted on ships are not covered by the Register?

The term "ground-to-air" in Category VII refers only to surface-to-air missiles that are mounted at fixed land sites or on wheeled or tracked mobile launchers. Surface-to-air missiles mounted on ships are covered by UNROCA. Also, MANPADS are included in Category VII as subcategory B (also see questions 20, 21, 23 and 24).

11.   Are States expected to report the exports or imports of components used in the assembly, co-production or upgrading of items associated with the categories covered by UNROCA or SALW?

No, the Register only records transfers of complete equipment, as defined in the seven categories, and SALW. If a component is imported by a State, which then uses this component to produce and export complete equipment covered by UNROCA, the export of the completed equipment should be reported.

12.   Complete equipment is sometimes exported or imported in disassembled components (known as "kits"). Should these be reported to UNROCA?

Strictly speaking, imports and exports of these kits do not need to be reported as transfers. However, States may do so if they wish, making clear that they are disassembled kits. Another option is for the importing State to supply background information on the equipment as procurement from national production once the kit is assembled on its territory.

13. How should items exported by a State other than the State of origin (manufacture) be reported?

The exporting State should report the transfer on the export form, indicating the State of origin in column D of the standardized form.

14. How should transfer of equipment to an intermediate location be reported?

If, for example, State A transfers air-to-air missiles to State B for installation on combat aircraft to be exported to State C, State A should report the export of missiles to State C and declare in column E of the form that State B is the intermediate location.

Example

In 2015, 72 GOAL-104A air-to-air missiles (AAM) and 72 STRIKE-S22 air-to-surface missiles (ASM), both with a range of 36 kilometres, were exported by State D for installation in State C and onward exportation to State Y. State C installed these missiles on F-19B multi-role fighter aircraft and then exported them to State Y in 2015.

Missiles from D to C

EXPORTS
Reports of international arms transfers
(According to United Nations General Assembly resolution 46/36 L)
Reporting country: D
Calendar year: 2015

A	B	C	D	E	REMARKS	
Category (I-VII)	Final importer State(s)	Number of items	State of origin if not exporter	Intermediate location (if any)	Description of item	Comments on the transfer
VII. (a) Missiles and missile launchers	1) Y 2) Y	72 72		C for re-export to Y		

Missiles from C to Y as part of combat aircraft export

EXPORTS
Reports of international arms transfers
(According to United Nations General Assembly resolution 46/36 L)
Reporting country: C
Calendar year: 2015

A	B	C	D	E	REMARKS	
Category (I-VII)	Final importer State(s)	Number of items	State of origin if not exporter	Intermediate location (if any)	Description of item	Comments on the transfer
VII. (a) Missiles and missile launchers	1) Y 2) Y	72 72	D D		1) AAM, type GOAL-104A 2) ASM, type STRIKE-S22 See Note 1.	

Note 1: In this case, State C chooses to supply additional data on the equipment in the remarks column.

15. Should transfer of second-hand equipment be reported?

Yes, all transfers relating to equipment included in the seven categories of UNROCA should be reported, regardless of whether the equipment is new or second-hand. The same applies for reporting on transfers of SALW.

16. Which State is to report the transfer of an item that was co-produced by three countries?

The transfer should be reported by the final exporting State of the complete equipment. Information concerning the co-production of the item could be given in column D and the "Remarks" section of the standardized form.

17. What weapons should be reported as SALW?

There are no commonly agreed international definitions of SALW. For the purposes of reporting to UNROCA, and bearing in mind its focus on military weapons, small arms include revolvers and self-loading pistols, rifles and carbines, sub-machine guns, assault rifles and light machine guns. Light weapons include heavy machine guns, hand-held under-barrel and mounted grenade launchers, portable anti-tank guns, portable anti-tank missile launchers and rocket systems, recoilless rifles and mortars of calibres less than 75 mm. These items are listed in the standardized forms for reporting exports and imports of SALW. In addition, Member States have the discretion to report other types of SALW using the lines labelled "Other" or the "Remarks" column in the forms.

Background information

Member States are invited to report to UNROCA information on their military holdings, procurement through national production and relevant policies and national legislation.

Provision of background information on **military holdings** relates to the number and type of items of equipment in active and reserve units or in storage. It serves as a key confidence-building measure.

Data and information on **procurement through national production** refer to the number and type of items of equipment produced within the State. Providing such data and information engenders the same degree of transparency from both States that procure weapons primarily though national production and from those that depend on imports of conventional arms.

Sharing information on **relevant policies and national legislation** increases the transparency of policies regarding production, acquisition and transfers of conventional armaments. This would only need to be provided with regard to policies/laws that have not been reported earlier.

Reporting forms: standardized, nil

All Member States are called upon to annually provide data on the number of items exported and imported in each of the seven categories of equipment and, for that purpose, to use the **standardized reporting form** through the UNROCA web-based reporting tool. A separate reporting form should be used for transfers of **SALW**.

Members States are encouraged to use the UNROCA web-based reporting tool in order to ensure immediate availability of data, to facilitate the management of UNROCA and to ensure accuracy of data included in the annual consolidated report of the Secretary-General.

Member States that have not processed any arms transfer in the relevant calendar year can submit a simple **nil report**, for which a form is also available. Nil reporting is important, as it allows for a truly global picture of the international transactions in equipment covered by UNROCA, thus enhancing the value of the Register as a confidence-building instrument. Nil reports can also be submitted through the web-based reporting tool.

Member States can submit a forward-looking "rolling nil" return for up to three years. This implies declaring a nil return to cover a period of up to three years of future reporting because the State has no plans to import or export conventional arms covered by the Register during the declared period. The United Nations Office for Disarmament Affairs will nevertheless send a note verbale to the Member State each year to request an update, if one is necessary. For example, if a Member State submits a rolling nil return in 2018, this Member State report will be valid for the years 2017, 2018 and 2019, unless the Member State indicates that an update is necessary.

In the case of an international arms transfer involving an export or import of **equipment from a State other than the State of manufacture**, the name of the country of manufacture should be entered in column D. In the case of an international arms transfer involving transport or retention of equipment to or in an intermediate location, the name of the intermediate location should be entered in column E. (For example, if a missile is exported for integration with a combat aircraft that is manufactured at an intermediate location, the intermediate location should be entered.)

The right-hand column on the form ("Remarks") contains two parts: "description of item" and "comments on the transfer". It is designed to offer Member States the opportunity to provide additional data on transfers, thus enhancing the quality of the information provided. As the provision for such information might be affected by security and other relevant concerns of Member States, this column should be filled in at Member States' discretion. To aid the understanding of the international transfers reported, Member States may wish to indicate the designation, type or model of equipment, or to use various descriptive elements contained in the definitions of categories I to VII, which also serve as guides to describe the transferred equipment. A Member State may use this column to provide any explanatory remarks it sees fit. (For example, the column could be used to indicate if a transfer involves obsolete or newly produced equipment.)[6]

The standardized form for reporting international transfers of SALW is similar in structure to the form for the seven categories of UNROCA. The exception is that column A of the SALW form contains two separate lists, one for five types of small arms and the other for six types of light weapons. As these lists are not comprehensive, the last line of each list is labelled "Other" and is intended to enable Member States to enter information on types of SALW not reflected in the lists.

Submitting a report to the Register

Each year, Member States should report their data for the previous year by 31 May to the United Nations Office for Disarmament Affairs (UNODA) through www.unroca.org/reporting/login. Access to the secure reporting platform is granted to each **national point of contact** by the UNODA. A list of national points of contact is available. To update information on a national point of contact, write to conventionalarms-unoda@un.org.

---

[6] The 2003 and 2006 Groups of Governmental Experts reaffirmed the view that use of the "Remarks" column helped in understanding the data submitted and added qualitatively to the information in the Register and thus, encouraged States in a position to do so to provide such information (see A/58/64, paras. 100 and 113 (c) and A/61/261, paras. 116 and 126 (d)).

Reports submitted by the 31 May deadline are included in the Secretary-General's annual consolidated report to the General Assembly containing the information received. Reports that are not submitted in time for inclusion in the annual consolidated report may be included in an addendum to this report. All reports, whether or not they are included in the consolidated report or the addendum, are posted on the UNROCA website.

Background information on military holdings and procurement through national production, as well as an index of other additional information, also appear in the Secretary-General's annual consolidated report or an addendum. States providing data on military holdings and procurement through national production may request that the data not be published.

Frequently asked questions

1. How are Member States requested to report to UNROCA?

At the beginning of each year, the United Nations Secretariat issues a "note verbale" to the Permanent Missions of all United Nations Member States, referencing the relevant General Assembly resolution on transparency in armaments and requesting each Member State to submit its report to UNROCA. States are also invited to provide data and information on additional background information.[7] Permanent Missions are expected to forward the note verbale to their relevant national ministry. Copies of the note verbale and the attachments can also be obtained directly from UNODA.

2. How should reports be submitted?

National points of contact should use the online reporting tool to submit their national reports. Contact UNODA for assistance: conventionalarms-unoda@un.org.

3. Why should States report on "national criteria on transfers"?

Member States are encouraged to explain their national criteria for defining a transfer. The explanatory note on the standardized reporting forms on export and import under note f provides guidance to that end. Information on criteria can also be provided at the bottom of the reporting forms under "National criteria on transfers". This information helps the authorities in a State to interpret the data provided by other States.

4. What if a State submits data on equipment that is not covered by UNROCA or with a physical measurement or projectile range less than the standard set by the definition for one of the categories? For example, suppose a State reports that it exported 30 ground-to-air missiles (specifically excluded from Category VII) or missiles with a range less than the reporting criteria of at least 25 kilometres.

Data submitted by a State using the format of the standardized form will be entered in UNROCA as submitted, even if it includes equipment outside the seven categories. The related report of the Secretary-General may indicate that the equipment falls outside the definitions.

---

[7] Member States have not approved a standardized form for submission of data and information on procurement through national production and on military holdings. However, in order to facilitate the submission of such information through the UNROCA online reporting tool, UNODA has developed enabling forms, which the 2016 Group of Governmental Experts has referred to as de facto forms (see p. "84. The Group recommends that the Secretary-General continue to invite Member States in a position to do so to provide data and information on procurement through national production to the Register as part of their additional background information. Member States providing such information are invited to use the de facto reporting form on procurement through national production. This does not preclude Member States from using any other method of reporting they deem appropriate." on page 48 (A/71/259, paras. 84 and 85)).

5.   What if a State, after evaluating its exports and imports of conventional arms, determines that it has none that fit the criteria for reporting?

States in this situation are invited to submit a nil report to UNROCA stating that no exports or imports have taken place in any of the seven categories or SALW during the previous year. The submission of a blank form without any clarification cannot be assumed to be a nil report. Member States will be given the option to submit a rolling nil report valid for a maximum of three years.

6.   When should a State submit a "rolling nil report"?

A Member State submitting a rolling nil return for up to three years is in fact declaring that it is in a position to cover up to three years of future reporting because it has no plans to import or export conventional arms covered by the "7+1" categories of the Register during the three-year period. UNODA will send a note verbale to the Member State each year to request if an update is necessary, but will utilize the rolling nil return for the period indicated by the Member State when recording this Member State's annual participation in the Register.

7.   What if a State submits a rolling nil report in 2017 but subsequently decides to import, in 2018, equipment covered under one or more of the seven categories of UNROCA or SALW?

The State in question should report the import of the equipment imported in 2018, overriding its rolling nil report that would cover 2018. Therefore, if the State does not engage in any transfer of relevant equipment in the following year, 2019 (which was initially covered by the rolling nil report), it should submit another nil report in 2019.

8.   Are States requested to submit details on the designation, model or type of the transferred weapons?

The "Remarks" column was designed to aid the understanding of international transfers by providing the opportunity, if States so wish, to report the designation, type or model of the equipment being transferred. The 2016 Group of Governmental Experts encouraged States to provide such information for all types of equipment reported. It is also recommended that this column be used to provide additional clarification of transfers, such as if the equipment is obsolete or the result of co-production.

Administration of the Register

Frequently asked questions

1.   When should data and information, including background information, be submitted to the United Nations?

States are asked to submit the requested data and information online by 31 May annually. For example, data for calendar year 2006 should be submitted by 31 May 2007. The data and information submitted will become part of UNROCA.

2.   What should a State do if, after submitting information for a certain calendar year, it determines that the information was incomplete or contained a technical error?

Sometimes, Member States seek corrections or clarification regarding technical errors or omissions in national reports. In such instances, States should provide written information referring to the item in question. There is no cut-off date for such corrections, but they should be submitted as early as possible to enable UNODA to process them before publication of the annual report of the Secretary-General. Otherwise, corrections would be issued as corrigendum to the Secretary-General's annual report. There are also situations where UNODA seeks clarification from Member States regarding data and information submitted, in order to ensure that the national reports are accurately reflected in the consolidated report of Secretary-General. In these cases, UNODA usually reaches out to the Permanent Missions in New York or the points of contact for assistance.

3.   What happens to the arms transfer data and the background information once they are submitted?

The information is made public in the Secretary-General's annual report to the General Assembly, which also indexes and reproduces the reports submitted on procurement through national production and military holdings. Information on national policies is only indexed in the annual report. UNODA keeps files of the original data and information submitted by Member States. The information provided via the online reporting tool is automatically entered into the UNROCA database. Any State may request its own original data, by disk or printed copy, at any time.

4.   What happens if a State reports on transfers on which it is not expected to report to UNROCA?

Such data and information would be kept in UNODA as part of the submission by that State. Depending on the type of data and information in question, UNODA may decide not to publish such information in the consolidated report of the Secretary-General. For instance, if a Member State reports transfers to or from a State that is not a member of the United Nations, such information will not be reflected in the report of the Secretary-General.

National points of contact: role and responsibilities

The national point of contact (PoC) is the service or individual designated by a Government for communication and liaison on UNROCA matters. For reasons of continuity, it should preferably be a service or unit, instead of an individual. A Member State is free to designate any service or unit for this task.

Various groups of governmental experts have stressed the importance for UNROCA of functioning national points of contact. Whenever the details of the national PoC change, the Member State should provide the new information to UNODA in a timely manner.

The main role of the PoCs at the national level is to facilitate timely and reliable reporting to UNROCA. By maintaining effective procedures for collecting and processing data, as well as generating awareness of the benefits of reporting, the PoCs can play a key role in

Before submitting a national report, national points of contact (PoCs) are encouraged to take up contact with PoCs of States with which an arms transfer has taken place during the reporting period. This may ensure a reduction in the number of reported transfers on which the exporting and importing States inadvertently provide conflicting information.

the success of the Register. Close cooperation between the PoCs and UNODA is therefore encouraged. Recognizing the importance of the PoCs, the 2016 Group of Governmental Experts provided guidance to assist PoCs in the discharge of their functions (see page 58 (annex IV to the report of the 2016 Group of Governmental Experts)).

UNODA maintains and updates the list of PoCs to ensure it can communicate regularly and directly with the PoCs on matters pertaining to UNROCA, in particular updates on data and information provided by Member States to the Register; new developments with regard to the online reporting tool and guidelines; assistance opportunities for training and capacity-building for national points of contact; and reminders for the submission of reports.

The list of PoCs is made available to Member States to enable direct communication between national points of contact to allow corroboration and clarification of data submitted, as well as for sharing information on national practices relating to reporting and participation in the Register.

Frequently asked questions

1. How does a PoC cooperate with the United Nations Secretariat?

UNODA acts as the secretariat of UNROCA. Cooperation between PoCs and UNODA could include assistance, training, coordination and the provision of a password for online reporting. UNODA will also facilitate networking of PoCs at the regional level and will assist in the promotion of good practices in the organization of reporting work. PoCs are encouraged to contact UNODA whenever they consider it necessary.

2. When should a PoC take up contact with other PoCs?

Before submitting a national report, PoCs are encouraged to contact PoCs of States with which an arms transfer has taken place during the reporting period. This may ensure a reduction in the number of reported transfers on which the exporting and importing States inadvertently provide conflicting information.

3. How should changes in a PoC be provided?

The standardized reporting forms on exports and imports, as well as the nil reporting form, contain a section that invites such information, including contact details. In addition, Member States are encouraged to directly provide the relevant officer in UNODA with any updates or changes in the PoCs.

Participation in UNROCA

Table 1. Western European and other States

Year of Secretary-General's report	2006	2007	2008	2009	2010	2011	2012	2013	2014	2015	2016	2017
Number of reports	30	30	29	27	26	27	24	26	22	22	14	12
1. Andorra	✓	✓		✓	✓	✓	✓	✓	✓	✓		
2. Australia	✓	✓	✓	✓	✓	✓	✓	✓	✓			
3. Austria	✓	✓	✓	✓	✓	✓		✓	✓	✓	✓	
4. Belgium	✓	✓	✓	✓	✓	✓	✓	✓	✓	✓	✓	
5. Canada	✓	✓	✓	✓	✓	✓		✓		✓	✓	
6. Cyprus	✓	✓	✓	✓		✓	✓	✓	✓	✓	✓	
7. Denmark	✓	✓	✓	✓	✓	✓	✓	✓	✓	✓	✓	
8. Finland	✓	✓	✓	✓	✓	✓	✓	✓	✓	✓		✓
9. France	✓	✓	✓	✓		✓	✓	✓	✓			
10. Germany	✓	✓	✓	✓	✓	✓	✓	✓	✓	✓	✓	✓
11. Greece	✓	✓	✓		✓	✓	✓	✓		✓		✓
12. Iceland	✓	✓	✓	✓	✓	✓	✓	✓	✓			
13. Ireland	✓	✓	✓	✓	✓	✓	✓	✓	✓	✓		
14. Israel	✓	✓	✓	✓	✓	✓	✓			✓		
15. Italy	✓	✓	✓	✓	✓	✓	✓		✓	✓		
16. Liechtenstein	✓	✓	✓	✓	✓	✓	✓	✓				
17. Luxembourg	✓	✓	✓					✓	✓	✓		✓
18. Malta	✓	✓	✓	✓	✓	✓	✓	✓				
19. Monaco	✓	✓	✓	✓	✓	✓		✓			✓	
20. Netherlands	✓	✓	✓	✓	✓	✓	✓	✓	✓	✓	✓	✓
21. New Zealand	✓	✓	✓	✓	✓							
22. Norway	✓	✓	✓	✓	✓	✓	✓	✓	✓	✓		
23. Portugal	✓	✓	✓	✓	✓	✓	✓	✓	✓	✓	✓	✓
24. San Marino	✓	✓	✓		✓	✓	✓	✓	✓			
25. Spain	✓	✓	✓	✓	✓	✓	✓	✓	✓	✓	✓	✓
26. Sweden	✓	✓	✓	✓	✓		✓	✓	✓	✓	✓	✓
27. Switzerland	✓	✓	✓	✓	✓	✓	✓	✓	✓	✓	✓	✓
28. Turkey	✓	✓	✓	✓		✓		✓	✓	✓		✓
29. United Kingdom	✓	✓	✓	✓	✓	✓	✓	✓	✓	✓	✓	✓
30. United States	✓	✓	✓	✓	✓	✓	✓	✓	✓	✓	✓	✓

Note: Data for 2017 reflect the number of reports submitted as at 20 September 2017.

Table 2. Eastern European States

Year of Secretary-General's report	2006	2007	2008	2009	2010	2011	2012	2013	2014	2015	2016	2017
Number of reports	21	22	22	19	19	22	17	20	20	19	17	15
1. Albania	✓	✓	✓		✓	✓	✓	✓	✓	✓	✓	✓
2. Armenia	✓	✓	✓	✓	✓	✓		✓				✓
3. Azerbaijan	✓	✓		✓	✓	✓	✓		✓			
4. Belarus	✓	✓	✓	✓	✓	✓	✓	✓	✓	✓	✓	✓
5. Bosnia and Herzegovina	✓	✓	✓	✓	✓	✓		✓	✓	✓	✓	✓
6. Bulgaria	✓	✓	✓	✓	✓	✓	✓	✓	✓	✓	✓	✓
7. Croatia	✓	✓	✓	✓		✓	✓	✓	✓	✓		
8. Czech Republic	✓	✓	✓	✓		✓	✓	✓	✓	✓	✓	✓
9. Estonia	✓	✓	✓	✓	✓	✓	✓	✓	✓	✓	✓	
10. Georgia	✓	✓	✓									
11. Hungary	✓	✓	✓	✓	✓	✓	✓	✓	✓	✓	✓	✓
12. Latvia	✓	✓	✓	✓	✓	✓		✓	✓	✓	✓	✓
13. Lithuania	✓	✓	✓	✓	✓	✓	✓	✓	✓	✓	✓	✓
14. Montenegro[a]			✓			✓	✓		✓	✓	✓	✓
15. Poland	✓	✓	✓	✓	✓	✓	✓	✓	✓	✓		
16. Republic of Moldova	✓	✓	✓	✓	✓	✓		✓	✓	✓		
17. Romania	✓	✓	✓	✓	✓	✓	✓	✓	✓	✓	✓	✓
18. Russian Federation	✓	✓	✓	✓	✓	✓	✓	✓	✓	✓	✓	✓
19. Serbia		✓	✓		✓	✓		✓	✓	✓	✓	✓
20. Slovakia	✓	✓	✓	✓	✓	✓	✓	✓	✓	✓	✓	✓
21. Slovenia	✓	✓	✓	✓	✓	✓	✓	✓	✓	✓	✓	
22. The former Yugoslav Republic of Macedonia	✓	✓	✓	✓	✓	✓	✓	✓			✓	
23. Ukraine	✓	✓	✓	✓	✓	✓	✓	✓	✓	✓	✓	✓

Note: Data for 2017 reflect the number of reports submitted as at 20 September 2017.

  [a] Montenegro has been a Member State since 2006.

Table 3. Latin American and Caribbean States

Year of Secretary-General's report	2006	2007	2008	2009	2010	2011	2012	2013	2014	2015	2016	2017
Number of reports	21	20	11	13	8	16	7	9	8	6	5	2
1. Antigua and Barbuda	✓	✓	✓	✓	✓	✓						
2. Argentina		✓	✓	✓	✓	✓	✓	✓	✓	✓	✓	✓
3. Bahamas		✓					✓					
4. Barbados												
5. Belize	✓	✓	✓	✓		✓						
6. Bolivia (Plurinational State of)	✓	✓		✓	✓							
7. Brazil	✓	✓	✓	✓	✓	✓		✓	✓	✓		
8. Chile	✓	✓	✓	✓	✓	✓	✓	✓	✓		✓	✓
9. Colombia			✓		✓	✓	✓					
10. Costa Rica	✓	✓		✓								
11. Cuba	✓	✓									✓	
12. Dominica												
13. Dominican Republic						✓						
14. Ecuador	✓					✓	✓					
15. El Salvador		✓	✓			✓	✓	✓	✓	✓	✓	
16. Grenada	✓		✓	✓		✓		✓	✓	✓		
17. Guatemala	✓	✓	✓									
18. Guyana	✓					✓						
19. Haiti		✓										
20. Honduras												
21. Jamaica	✓	✓						✓		✓		
22. Mexico	✓	✓	✓	✓	✓	✓	✓	✓	✓	✓	✓	
23. Nicaragua	✓	✓										
24. Panama		✓		✓								
25. Paraguay	✓	✓										
26. Peru				✓	✓	✓						
27. Saint Kitts and Nevis	✓											
28. Saint Lucia	✓	✓										
29. Saint Vincent and Grenadines	✓	✓		✓								
30. Suriname	✓	✓	✓	✓		✓						
31. Trinidad and Tobago	✓	✓				✓		✓	✓	✓		
32. Uruguay						✓		✓	✓	✓	✓	
33. Venezuela (Bolivarian Republic of)												

Note: Data for 2017 reflect the number of reports submitted as at 20 September 2017.

Table 4. Asia and Pacific States

Year of Secretary-General's report	2006	2007	2008	2009	2010	2011	2012	2013	2014	2015	2016	2017
Number of reports	27	26	21	18	16	19	11	13	10	6	11	5
1. Afghanistan												
2. Bahrain												
3. Bangladesh	✓	✓	✓	✓		✓						
4. Bhutan		✓	✓	✓		✓		✓	✓		✓	
5. Brunei Darussalam		✓	✓									
6. Cambodia					✓	✓		✓	✓			
7. China		✓	✓	✓	✓	✓	✓	✓	✓	✓	✓	✓
8. Democratic People's Republic of Korea												
9. Fiji		✓	✓								✓	
10. India	✓	✓	✓	✓	✓	✓	✓	✓		✓	✓	
11. Indonesia	✓		✓	✓								
12. Iran (Islamic Republic of)												
13. Iraq												
14. Japan	✓	✓	✓	✓	✓	✓	✓	✓	✓	✓	✓	✓
15. Jordan	✓		✓									
16. Kazakhstan	✓	✓		✓	✓		✓	✓	✓	✓		
17. Kiribati	✓	✓										
18. Kuwait	✓											
19. Kyrgyzstan	✓		✓		✓							
20. Lao People's Democratic Republic					✓							
21. Lebanon	✓	✓	✓	✓	✓	✓			✓			✓
22. Malaysia	✓	✓		✓	✓	✓	✓	✓				
23. Maldives	✓	✓	✓				✓					
24. Marshall Islands	✓											
25. Micronesia (Federated States of)	✓	✓										
26. Mongolia	✓	✓	✓			✓				✓	✓	
27. Myanmar												
28. Nauru	✓	✓	✓	✓	✓			✓			✓	
29. Nepal								✓				
30. Oman												
31. Pakistan[a]	✓	✓	✓	✓		✓		✓	✓	✓		
32. Palau	✓	✓	✓			✓					✓	
33. Papua New Guinea												
34. Philippines		✓		✓					✓			
35. Qatar									✓			

Year of Secretary-General's report	2006	2007	2008	2009	2010	2011	2012	2013	2014	2015	2016	2017
Number of reports	27	26	21	18	16	19	11	13	10	6	11	5
36. Republic of Korea	✓	✓	✓	✓	✓	✓	✓	✓	✓			
37. Samoa	✓	✓	✓	✓	✓	✓	✓					
38. Saudi Arabia												
39. Singapore	✓	✓	✓	✓	✓	✓	✓	✓		✓	✓	✓
40. Solomon Islands	✓	✓		✓		✓						
41. Sri Lanka												
42. Syrian Arab Republic												
43. Tajikistan	✓	✓	✓	✓	✓	✓						
44. Thailand	✓				✓	✓	✓					
45. Timor-Leste												
46. Tonga		✓										
47. Turkmenistan	✓					✓						
48. Tuvalu	✓	✓										
49. United Arab Emirates												
50. Uzbekistan												
51. Vanuatu	✓									✓	✓	
52. Viet Nam	✓	✓	✓	✓	✓	✓	✓	✓	✓	✓	✓	✓
53. Yemen												

Note: Data for 2017 reflect the number of reports submitted as at 20 September 2017.

[a] Submitted its 2014 and 2015 report in 2017.

Table 5. African States

Year of Secretary-General's report	2006	2007	2008	2009	2010	2011	2012	2013	2014	2015	2016	2017
Number of reports	16	15	8	4	4	2	2	3	1	1	0	0
1. Algeria												
2. Angola												
3. Benin												
4. Botswana												
5. Burkina Faso	✓	✓										
6. Burundi	✓			✓								
7. Cameroon												
8. Cabo Verde												
9. Central African Republic												
10. Chad												
11. Comoros	✓				✓			✓				
12. Congo												
13. Côte d'Ivoire												
14. Democratic Republic of the Congo												
15. Djibouti	✓	✓	✓									
16. Egypt												
17. Equatorial Guinea												
18. Eritrea												
19. Ethiopia												
20. Gabon		✓										
21. Gambia		✓										
22. Ghana			✓									
23. Guinea												
24. Guinea-Bissau												
25. Kenya	✓	✓	✓									
26. Lesotho	✓											
27. Liberia												
28. Libya												
29. Madagascar						✓a						
30. Malawi												
31. Mali		✓										
32. Mauritania												
33. Mauritius	✓		✓		✓			✓				
34. Morocco												
35. Mozambique	✓	✓					✓					
36. Namibia	✓	✓	✓									

Year of Secretary-General's report	2006	2007	2008	2009	2010	2011	2012	2013	2014	2015	2016	2017
Number of reports	16	15	8	4	4	2	2	3	1	1	0	0
37. Niger	✓											
38. Nigeria												
39. Rwanda												
40. Sao Tome and Principe												
41. Senegal	✓	✓								✓		
42. Seychelles	✓	✓		✓								
43. Sierra Leone	✓	✓										
44. Somalia												
45. South Africa	✓	✓	✓	✓	✓	✓	✓	✓	✓			
46. South Sudan[b]												
47. Sudan												
48. Swaziland		✓	✓	✓								
49. Togo		✓	✓									
50. Tunisia					✓							
51. Uganda												
52. United Republic of Tanzania	✓											
53. Zambia	✓	✓										
54. Zimbabwe												

Note: Data for 2017 reflect the number of reports submitted as at 20 September 2017.

[a] Submitted in 2012.

[b] South Sudan has been a Member State since 2011.

Part 2

A/71/259

Report on the continuing operation of the United Nations Register of Conventional Arms and its further development

Summary

The report of the 2016 Group of Governmental Experts on the continuing operation and further development of the United Nations Register of Conventional Arms updates the Register's definitions and recommends ways to increase its relevance for States and to enable greater participation. The Group made progress on the issue of the status of small arms and light weapons in the Register, which had been discussed by previous groups of governmental experts since 2000. The Group recommends that the Secretary-General appeal to Member States to report international transfers of small arms and light weapons in parallel with the seven categories of the Register, on a trial basis, using a separate reporting form for international transfers of those weapons. The results of the trial are intended to inform the deliberations of the next Group of Governmental Experts on whether to expand the Register to include an eighth category for small arms and light weapons.

The Group discussed a number of proposals concerning adjustments to the current seven categories of weapons covered by the Register. The Group recommends a new description and heading for category IV to include unmanned combat aerial vehicles as a subcategory, with the heading amended to read "Combat aircraft and unmanned combat aerial vehicles".

The Group expressed serious concern at the decline in reporting to the Register since 2008 and, in order to better understand the reasons for such a decline, the Group developed a questionnaire to be completed by Member States on their national reporting systems and reporting challenges. Given that the decline in "nil" return submissions corresponds with the overall decline in reporting to the Register, the Group recommends that Member States that do not have plans to procure items covered by the Register's categories for several years can provide a rolling "nil" return, which can be valid for up to a maximum of three years. The Group recognized the contribution to confidence-building by Member States that report authorizations of exports and imports when data on actual exports and imports are not available. The Group stressed the importance of Member States designating a national point of contact for the Register, and provided practical guidance for increasing their effectiveness.

The report notes that the twenty-fifth anniversary of the Register's establishment should be celebrated in recognition of its role not only in increasing global transparency in international arms transfers, but as a point of reference and inspiration for other regional and international confidence-building mechanisms, and as an important element in the contribution of the United Nations to international peace and security. The Group noted that the occasion would also provide an opportunity to promote greater participation in the Register. The Group recommends that the translation of the online reporting tool for the electronic filing of submissions into all official languages of the United Nations be a priority for the continuing operation of the Register.

Foreword by the Secretary-General

Established in 1992, the United Nations Register of Conventional Arms serves as a global instrument to promote transparency and international stability by building trust among States in the transfer of conventional arms in seven categories.

Persistent security challenges in many parts of the world underscore the continued relevance of the Register and the need to adapt it to emerging technological realities.

The 2016 review of the Register was undertaken by a group of governmental experts from 15 States and addresses recent challenges and threats. Specifically, the Group examined the destabilizing accumulation of illicit small arms and the increased military use of armed unmanned aerial vehicles.

The Group recommends that Member States apply, on a trial basis, a reporting formula that includes international transfers of small arms. This would replace the current practice of reporting such transfers as part of additional background information.

This recommendation constitutes a step towards the goal of including small arms as an eighth category of the Register and seeks to respond to the growing security concerns arising from the diversion of small arms. The Group also recommends broadening the title and definition of category V of the Register, which currently covers (manned) combat aircraft, to include unmanned combat aerial vehicles. This recommendation will enable the Register to keep pace with the increasing trends in international transfers of unmanned combat aerial vehicles.

I thank the Chair of the Group and the experts for their important work. I count on Member States to take into account the recommendations of the Group in the continued operation of the Register as a dynamic instrument in our shared efforts to promote international security.

Letter of transmittal

22 July 2016

I have the honour to submit herewith the report of the Group of Governmental Experts on the continuing operation of the United Nations Register of Conventional Arms and its further development, which you appointed pursuant to paragraph 6 (b) of General Assembly resolution 68/43. The Group held two sessions of work in Geneva (4-8 April 2016 and 11-15 July 2016) and one in New York (16-20 May 2016).

The establishment of the Group is part of the triennial review of the Register, which aims at ensuring that the Register adapts to changes in the international security environment and to new developments in weapons technology, thereby safeguarding its continued relevance as a reporting instrument and confidence-building mechanism.

The Group built on the work carried out by previous Groups of Governmental Experts and, additionally, explored new areas for the further development of the Register. The Group's report reflects the intensive discussions that took place during its three sessions of work, which resulted in recommendations that constitute appreciable steps forward in several areas, including on issues considered by previous Groups of Governmental Experts.

In particular, the Group recommends that Member States apply, on a trial basis, a seven plus one formula for reporting on their international transfers of small arms and light weapons, rather than the current practice of reporting such transfers as part of additional background information. This recommendation seeks to respond to the concerns of many Member States for which the diversion of small arms and light weapons poses a serious threat to both security and socioeconomic development. It constitutes progress towards a possible inclusion of small arms and light weapons as an eighth category in the Register.

In addition, the Group recommends a further expansion of the scope of the instrument by broadening the title and the definition of category V of the Register, which currently covers (manned) combat aircraft, to also include unmanned combat aerial vehicles. This recommendation will allow the Register to encompass the growing volume of international transfers of unmanned combat aerial vehicles.

The Group also made recommendations aimed at exploring synergies between the Register and other existing transparency instruments; enhancing the effectiveness of national points of contact; increasing the stability of national reporting mechanisms; and strengthening support for the Register by the Office for Disarmament Affairs of the Secretariat.

I would like to thank the Group for electing me to serve as its Chair, and I commend all the members of the Group for their hard work and for the constructive and responsible manner in which they discharged the task entrusted to us. On behalf of us all, I would also like to thank the High Representative for Disarmament Affairs, Mr. Kim Won-soo, for his encouragement and advice, the Office for Disarmament Affairs, not least Mr. António Évora, for the excellent support provided, and Dr. Paul Holtom for his indispensable contributions as consultant to the Group.

Finally, Mr. Secretary-General, on behalf of myself and the Group, I would like to thank you for the trust you have placed in us and for giving us this opportunity to contribute to the international community's efforts to promote transparency in armaments.

The Group comprised the following experts:

Austria
Mr. George-Wilhelm Gallhofer (second and third sessions)
Counsellor, Permanent Mission of Austria to the United Nations, New York

Bulgaria
Ms. Lachezara Stoeva
Counsellor, Permanent Mission of Bulgaria to the United Nations, New York

Chile
Mr. Pablo Castro (first and third sessions)
International Security Adviser, Directorate of International and Human Security,
Ministry of Foreign Affairs, Santiago

Mr. Juan Pablo Rosso (second session)
International Security Adviser, Directorate of International and Human Security,
Ministry of Foreign Affairs, Santiago

China
Mr. Liu Wei
Director, Department of Arms Control, Ministry of Foreign Affairs, Beijing

Colombia
Mr. Raul Esteban Sanchez Niño
Disarmament and International Security, Ministry of Foreign Affairs, Bogota

France
Ms. Stéphanie Laverny
Chief of Section, Directorate-General for International Relations and Strategy,
Ministry of Defence, Paris

Germany
Mr. Thomas Göbel (first session)
Head, Division for Conventional Disarmament and Arms Control, Ministry of Foreign
Affairs, Berlin

Mr. Tarmo Hannes Dix (second and third sessions)
Division for Conventional Disarmament and Arms Control, Ministry of Foreign Affairs,
Berlin

Kazakhstan
Major Arnyr Ajzhigitov
Chief of the Directorate of the Centre for Arms Control, Ministry of Defence, Astana

Republic of Korea
Ms. Kim Kyoung Hae (first and third sessions)
Second Secretary, Permanent Mission of the Republic of Korea to the United Nations Office
at Geneva

Ms. Yoon Seoungmee (second session)
Counsellor, Permanent Mission of the Republic of Korea to the United Nations, New York

Nigeria
Mr. Abiodun Richards Adejola (second session)
Minister, Permanent Mission of Nigeria to the United Nations, New York

Russian Federation
Mr. Vladislav Antoniuk
Deputy Director, Department for Non-Proliferation and Arms Control,
Ministry of Foreign Affairs, Moscow

Singapore
Colonel Foo Khee Loon
Military Adviser, Permanent Mission of Singapore to the United Nations, New York

Sweden
Mr. Paul Beijer
Ambassador, Department for Disarmament and Non-proliferation,
Ministry of Foreign Affairs, Stockholm

Trinidad and Tobago
Ms. Charlene Roopnarine (second session)
First Secretary, Permanent Mission of Trinidad and Tobago to the United Nations,
New York

United Kingdom of Great Britain and Northern Ireland
Mr. Guy Pollard
Deputy Permanent Representative to the Conference on Disarmament, Geneva

United States of America
Mr. William Malzahn
Senior Coordinator for the Arms Trade Treaty, Office of Conventional Arms Threat
Reduction, Bureau of International Security and Non-proliferation,
United States Department of State, Washington D.C.

(Signed) Paul **Beijer**
Chair, Group of Governmental Experts
on the United Nations Register of Conventional Arms

I.   Introduction

A.   Establishment of the Register

1.   The General Assembly, in its resolution 46/36 L entitled "Transparency in armaments", requested the Secretary-General to establish and maintain a universal and non-discriminatory Register of Conventional Arms. The objective of the Register is to prevent excessive and destabilizing accumulation of arms in order to enhance confidence, promote stability, help States to exercise restraint, ease tensions and strengthen regional and international peace and security (resolution 46/36 L, paras. 1 and 2). Member States were called upon to provide annually for the Register data on exports and imports of conventional arms in the seven categories covered by the Register, and were invited to include information on military holdings, procurement through national production and relevant national policies, pending the expansion of its scope.

2.   Pursuant to that resolution, the Secretary-General convened a Panel of Governmental Technical Experts in 1992 to bring the Register into operation. Endorsing the recommendations of the Panel (see A/47/342 and Corr.1), the General Assembly called upon all Member States to provide the requested data and information to the Secretary-General annually, beginning in 1993 (resolution 47/52 L).

B.   Review of the Register

3.   In its resolution 46/36 L, the General Assembly decided to look at the Register's future expansion and to keep the scope of and participation in the Register under review, which is also reflected in the 1992 report of the Panel of Governmental Technical Experts. As a result, the Register has been periodically reviewed, thus far at three-year intervals, with the exception of the 2013 Group of Governmental Experts, which was convened four years after the 2009 Group of Governmental Experts.

4.   The 2016 Group of Governmental Experts noted that it was meeting to review the continuing operation and further development of the Register on the twenty-fifth anniversary of the publication in 1991 of the study by the Group of Experts on ways and means of promoting transparency in international transfers of conventional arms (A/46/301) and the adoption of General Assembly resolution 46/36 L on 9 December 1991. The Group agreed that the Register had made a significant contribution to increasing transparency in international transfers of conventional arms during the past 25 years, and that 170 Member States had participated in the Register at least once. It is estimated that around 90 per cent of the world's international transfers of conventional arms are reported to the Register. The Register also serves as a point of reference and inspiration for regional and international confidence-building mechanisms and arms control and transfer control instruments. It is an important element in the contribution of the United Nations to international peace and security.

1994-2009 groups of governmental experts

5.   The General Assembly took note of the report of the 1994 Group of Governmental Experts (A/49/316) and decided to keep the scope of and participation in the Register under review, requesting Member States to provide the Secretary-General with their views in that regard, as well as on transparency measures related to weapons of mass destruction. The recommendations contained in the Group of Governmental Experts report were endorsed by the General Assembly in its resolution 49/75 C.

6.   The 1997 Group of Governmental Experts continued to elaborate on technical procedures to ensure the effective operation of the Register. It proposed extending the

reporting deadline from 30 April to 31 May, and encouraged the submission of information on national points of contact and the use of the "Remarks" column in the reporting format (see A/52/316). It also recommended the inclusion of information, provided on a voluntary basis, on procurement through national production and on military holdings in the annual reports of the Secretary-General to the General Assembly. The recommendations contained in the Group of Governmental Experts report were endorsed by the Assembly in its resolution 53/77 V.

7.   The 2000 Group of Governmental Experts recommended, with a view to encouraging greater participation in the Register, the holding of regional and subregional workshops and seminars with the assistance of interested Member States; the introduction of a simplified form for providing "nil" returns; and the updating of the information booklet on the United Nations Register of Conventional Arms (see A/55/281). The 2000 Group agreed that the Register covered conventional arms only and therefore the question of transparency with respect to weapons of mass destruction was an issue that should be addressed by the General Assembly. The recommendations contained in the Group of Governmental Experts report were endorsed by the Assembly in its resolution 57/75.

8.   The 2003 Group of Governmental Experts concluded that considerable progress had been made towards achieving a relatively high level of participation in the Register (see A/58/274). It recommended lowering the reporting threshold of large-calibre artillery systems from 100 mm to 75 mm in category III, and the inclusion, on an exceptional basis, of man-portable air-defence systems as a subcategory in category VII, "Missiles and missile launchers". In addition, it noted that Member States who were in a position to do so could provide additional background information on international transfers of small arms and light weapons made or modified to military specifications and intended for military use. The recommendations were endorsed by the General Assembly in its resolution 58/54.

9.   The 2006 Group of Governmental Experts recommended that the reporting threshold of "Warships" under category VI should be reduced from 750 to 500 metric tons (see A/61/261). With regard to international transfers of small arms and light weapons, the Group recommended that Member States in a position to do so should provide additional background information and utilize the optional standardized reporting form developed by the Group of Governmental Experts. The 2006 Group also began to discuss the issue of reporting the international transfer of armed unmanned aerial vehicles in the context of the Register. The recommendations were endorsed by the General Assembly in its resolution 61/77.

10.   The 2009 Group of Governmental Experts recommended that efforts should continue to ensure the Register's relevance for all regions and enhance the universal participation by Member States (see A/64/296). In particular, the Group recommended that measures should be undertaken to assist Member States to build capacity for the submission of meaningful reports, including on small arms and light weapons, and made adjustments to the standardized reporting forms. Furthermore, it recommended that the Secretary-General seek the views of Member States on whether the continued absence of small arms and light weapons as a main category in the Register had limited the relevance of the Register, thereby directly affecting decisions on the participation of Member States in the instrument. The Group continued the discussion on reporting international transfers of armed unmanned aerial vehicles. The recommendations were endorsed by the General Assembly in its resolution 64/54.

2013 Group of Governmental Experts

11.   The General Assembly, in its resolution 66/39, requested the Secretary-General to prepare a report on the continuing operation of the Register and its further development with the assistance of a Group of Governmental Experts to be convened in 2012, taking into account

the views expressed by Member States and the reports of the Secretary-General on this issue. Pursuant to General Assembly decision 67/517, the Group of Governmental Experts was convened in 2013, without change to the other modalities for the Group as set forth in resolution 66/39.

12. The 2013 Group of Governmental Experts recommended that Member States reporting international transfers of armed unmanned aerial vehicles should do so using categories IV and V of the Register (see A/68/140). It repeated the recommendation by the 2009 Group of Governmental Experts that the Secretary-General should seek the views of Member States on whether the continued absence of small arms and light weapons as a main category in the Register had limited the relevance of the Register and directly affected decisions on participation. It also strongly recommended enhanced budgetary support and human resources from within the Conventional Arms Branch of the Office for Disarmament Affairs for the maintenance and promotion of the Register. The Group encouraged Member States in a position to do so to provide voluntary contributions to the Register's secretariat and to render assistance, upon request, to Member States to build capacity to submit reports to the Register. The recommendations were endorsed by the General Assembly in its resolution 68/43.

2016 Group of Governmental Experts

13. The 2016 Group of Governmental Experts was established pursuant to General Assembly resolution 68/43, which requested the Secretary-General to prepare a report on the continuing operation of the Register and its further development, taking into account the work of the Conference on Disarmament, relevant deliberations within the United Nations, views expressed by Member States and the reports of the Secretary-General on this issue.

II. Review of the continuing operation of the Register

A. General

14. The Group reviewed the data and information submitted by Member States to the Register for the calendar years 1992-2015 and tables and graphs with statistical data compiled by the Office for Disarmament Affairs. The Group benefited from non-papers provided by governmental experts, a background paper prepared by the Office for Disarmament Affairs, and presentations by the Office, the Organization for Security and Cooperation in Europe (OSCE), the Bundeswehr Verification Unit and Coventry University. The Group complemented its deliberations with this information to develop conclusions and recommendations for improving the relevance of and promoting universal participation in the Register.

B. Relevance and universality of the Register

15. The Group considered the relevance of the Register for the security concerns of all Member States, addressing this issue in connection with the goal of universality of the Register. The Group emphasized that the Register was an important instrument for building confidence and trust between States. It could help Member States to identify excessive and destabilizing accumulation of conventional arms, thereby informing decisions to limit risks that such accumulations could pose for international peace and security and contributing to conflict prevention.

16. In discussing relevance and universality, the Group considered whether the following issues affected participation in the Register: (a) that the information in the Register is not relevant for addressing the security concerns of all Member States and regions; (b) the omission from the Register of certain categories of conventional arms, in particular small arms and light

weapons; (c) that the Register is inherently discriminatory because it requests Member States to provide information on only one method for acquiring conventional weapons (import), but only invites Member States to provide information on procurement from national production; and (d) that some Member States face technical and bureaucratic challenges with regard to the control, record-keeping and reporting of international transfers of conventional arms. The Group decided that experts and the Secretariat should actively seek the views of Member States on the relevance of the Register and on barriers for achieving universality, in preparation for the deliberations of the next Group of Governmental Experts.

C.   Extent of participation

17.   The level of participation in the Register has declined significantly since 2008. The lowest level of reporting was recorded in 2012, when 52 Member States provided a report; 69 Member States reported in 2013, 59 in 2014, and 54 in 2015. The Secretariat also provided information on adherence by Member States to the annual 31 May deadline: 21 of 69 Member States reported by 31 May in 2013; 16 of 59 Member States by 31 May in 2014; 21 of 54 Member States by 31 May in 2015; and 27 reports had been submitted by 31 May in 2016.

18.   The Group noted that the General Assembly resolution on transparency in armaments regularly receives the support of three quarters of the Member States, with 156 Member States voting in favour of its adoption in 2011 and 154 in 2013. No Member State has voted against a General Assembly resolution on the Register. Of the 163 Member States that have voted at least once in support of resolutions on transparency in armaments for 2011 and 2013, 69 did not report to the Register during the years 2011-2015. Of these 69 Member States, 39 had reported at least once during the years 2005-2010, 22 had reported at least once during 1993-2004 and 8 have never reported to the Register. The Group therefore sought to identify the factors that could account for the discrepancy between the consistently high level of support for the Register in the Assembly and the decline in reporting.

19.   The General Assembly resolution on transparency in armaments was co-sponsored by 96 Member States in 2011; 72 of those 96 Member States co-sponsored the resolution in 2013. Of those 96 Member States, 24 did not report to the Register during the years 2011-2015. Of those 24 Member States, 17 reported at least once during 2005-2010, 6 reported at least once during 1993-2004 and 1 co-sponsor has never reported.

D.   "Nil" returns

20.   The Group noted the correlation between the number of Member States submitting a "nil" return and the level of overall reporting to the Register. The Group reviewed the 2012-2015 years of reporting, the years for which the level of overall reporting to the Register has been the lowest. These are also the years in which the proportion of "nil" returns has been the lowest overall: 25 per cent of reports submitted in 2012 were "nil" returns, 34 per cent in 2013, 31 per cent in 2014 and 26 per cent in 2015 (see figure I). This represents a significant drop from 2007, when 53 per cent of the 113 submissions were "nil" returns.

Figure I
Provision of "nil" returns to the Register, 2012-2015

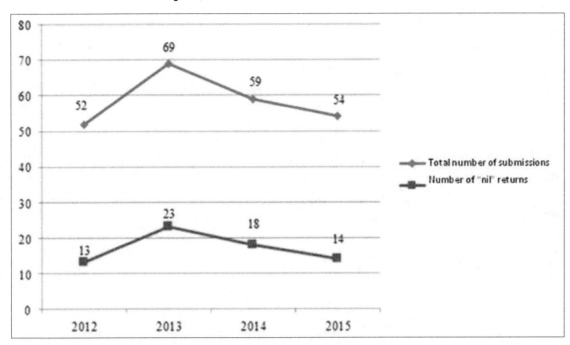

21.   The Group discussed the importance of "nil" returns for achieving the goal of universal participation in the Register. It recognized that "nil" returns were as important as returns containing information on imports and exports for building confidence and trust between Member States. The Group therefore considered different options, including rolling "nil" returns, to increase participation in the Register and facilitate the provision of "nil" returns.

E.   Reports on exports and imports

22.   The level of reporting exports of the seven categories of the conventional arms to the Register in the years 2012-2015 was consistent with the level during 2008-2011. An annual average of 31 Member States reported exports during 2012-2015 (see figure II). The annual average number of Member States reporting imports to the Register during 2012-2015 was 27, lower than the annual average of 42 Member States during 2008-2011.

Figure II
Reports on exports and imports, 2012-2015

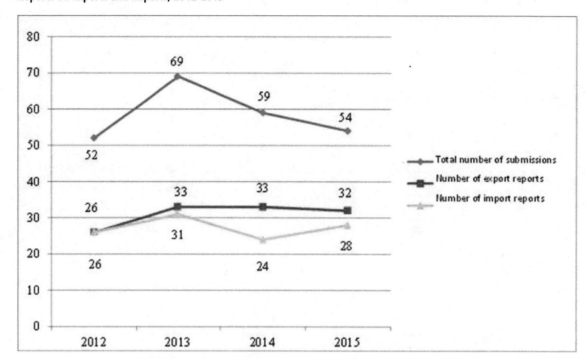

Note: A Member State's submission can consist of one of the following combinations: (a) both an export and an import report; (b) an export report and a "nil" return for imports; (c) an import report and a "nil" return for exports; or (d) a "nil" return for both imports and exports. Therefore, the combined number of import reports and export reports will not equal the total number of submissions.

F.   Reports on additional background information

23.   The level of reporting of additional background information mirrored the overall trend in reporting. The number of Member States reporting additional background information on military holdings during the years 2012-2015 is at a level comparable with the period considered by the 2013 Group of Governmental Experts (see figure III). The number of Member States providing additional background information on procurement through national production and international transfers of small arms and light weapons during 2012-2015 was lower than during 2008-2011.

24.   Since 1992, 54 Member States have provided additional background information on military holdings at least once. In 2012, 38 per cent of total submissions included additional background information on military holdings, with 36 per cent in 2013, 37 per cent in 2014 and 46 per cent in 2015 (see figure III). The number of Member States (25) that provided additional background information on military holdings in 2013 and 2015 is comparable with the level for the years 2008-2011.

25.   Since 1992, 48 Member States have provided additional background information on procurement through national production at least once. An annual average of 10 Member States provided additional background information on procurement through national production during the years 2012-2015, a notable drop from the annual average of 21 Member States that provided such information during 2008-2011 (see figure III). Of the submissions provided in 2012, 19 per cent contained background information on military holdings; that figure was 16 per cent in 2013, 17 per cent in 2014 and 19 per cent in 2015.

Figure III
Provision of additional background information, 2012-2015

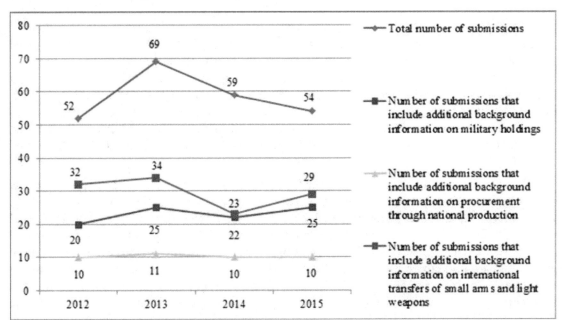

26.   Since 2003, 88 Member States have provided additional background information on international transfers of small arms and light weapons at least once. An annual average of 30 Member States provided additional background information on international transfers of small arms and light weapons during 2012-2015 (see figure III), a drop from the annual average of 44 Member States that provided such information during 2008-2011. In 2012, 62 per cent of submissions included background information on international transfers of small arms and light weapons; that figure was 49 per cent in 2013, 39 per cent in 2014 and 54 per cent in 2015.

27.   Based on the recommendation of the 2013 Group of Governmental Experts (A/68/140, para. 70), in its resolution 68/43 the General Assembly requested Member States to submit their views to the Secretary-General on the continuing operation of the Register and its further development, including on whether the absence of small arms and light weapons as a main category in the Register had limited the relevance of the Register and directly affected decisions on participation. China, Germany, Jamaica, Lebanon, Qatar and the European Union provided their views in response to that request during the period 2013-2015.

G.   Assessment of reporting at the regional level

28.   All regional groups of Member States recorded a decline in reporting to the Register during the years 2012-2015 compared with 2008-2011 (see figure IV). The level of reporting varied considerably between regional groups. Eastern European and Western European and other States have the highest levels of participation in the Register since its inception and during the years 2012-2015. However, both regions recorded their lowest level of participation in the Register in 2012, when 16 of the 23 Eastern European Member States and 18 of the 30 Western European and other States participated in the Register. The Group of Governmental Experts noted that Member States in those regional groups participate in various regional and multilateral information exchanges and transparency instruments relating to international transfers of conventional arms, and are therefore accustomed to regular reporting on items covered by the Register. For example, all European Member States from the group of Western European and

other States and all Eastern European Member States participate in OSCE, and therefore have politically binding reporting commitments to exchange their Register submission and reports on imports and exports of small arms and light weapons involving other OSCE participating States through OSCE.

29. Participation by Latin American and Caribbean Member States has dropped considerably from 16 of the region's 33 States in 2011 to 6 States in 2012 (see figure IV). Reporting has been consistent during the years 2013-2015, with nine Member States reporting in 2013 and eight in 2014 and 2015. This is well below the peak reporting year of 2002, when 26 Member States from the region reported. The Group of Governmental Experts was informed that participation in the Organization of American States Inter-American Convention on Transparency in Conventional Weapons Acquisitions had also declined during the period 2012-2015.

30. The level of reporting by Member States in Asia and the Pacific was particularly low during the years 2012-2015 compared with reporting levels before 2011. The annual average number of reports submitted during 2012-2015 was 10, down from 19 for 2008-2011 (see figure IV). In 2013, 13 Member States reported, representing 25 per cent of the region, compared with only 8 Member States in 2015, representing 15 per cent of the region. Member States in Central Asia are participating States in OSCE, and therefore have politically binding reporting commitments to exchange through OSCE their Register submission and reports on imports and exports of small arms and light weapons involving other OSCE participating States. The 2013 Group of Governmental Experts called for particular attention to be paid to encouraging reporting in the Middle East. Only Lebanon and Qatar provided information to the Register from this subregion during the years 2012-2015.

31. Africa has consistently recorded the lowest number and share of Member States reporting to the Register for any region. No African Member State reported to the Register in 2015 (see figure IV). The annual average number of Member States that reported during the years 2012-2015 was one, compared with five during 2008-2011. The level of reporting has thus dropped significantly from a high of 17 Member States in 2001 and 2003.

Figure IV
Percentage of Member States that have reported to the Register during the years 2012-2015, by regional group

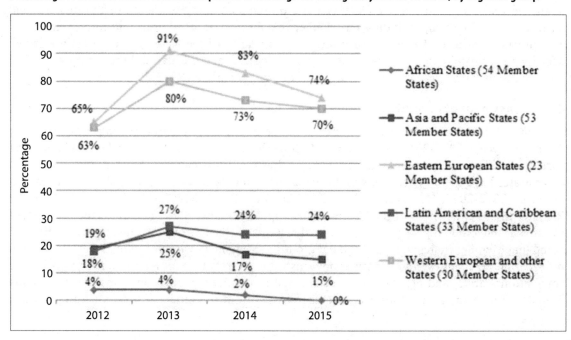

H.   Access to data and information reported

32.   The Group stressed the importance of making information provided to the Register available in a timely manner and easily accessible. Experts were provided with an opportunity to review the new Register website (Transparency in the global reported arms trade at www.unroca. org/). The new database provides an interface for comparing data on conventional arms exports and imports submitted by Member States since the beginning of the operation of the Register, as well as access to additional background information provided by Member States. It is also possible to compare data submitted by Member States on exports and imports of small arms and light weapons. Data on imports and procurement through national production are presented together, where available, to help identify potentially excessive and destabilizing accumulations. The website also hosts all annual submissions. The Group once again commended the Secretariat for its efforts to overhaul the Register's online database using limited resources.

33.   The Group noted that the United Nations, including the Security Council, and United Nations agencies, utilized the Register and its data to support efforts to promote peace, security and stability. The Group also discussed whether the data provided by Member States to the Register could contribute towards achieving target 4 of Sustainable Development Goal 16 of the 2030 Agenda for Sustainable Development.

34.   The Group noted that information provided by Member States to the Register continued to be utilized not only by Member States and the United Nations for trust and confidence-building, but also in peace and conflict analysis conducted by regional and international organizations, academic researchers, non-governmental organizations and the media. The Secretariat should continue to raise awareness of the Register among a broad range of interested parties.

I.   National points of contact

35.   A total of 146 Member States have supplied information on national points of contact at least once. Of the 73 Member States that reported to the Register in the years 2013-2015, 50 provided information on national points of contact. The Group paid particular attention to the issue of ensuring that information on national points of contact was up-to-date to facilitate the exchange of relevant information and enable bilateral consultations to build trust and confidence. The Group considered guidance for increasing the role and responsibilities of the national points of contact, as well as the role of permanent missions in New York.

J.   Role of the Secretariat

36.   The Group welcomed the response of the Conventional Arms Branch of the Office for Disarmament Affairs to the recommendations contained in the report of the 2013 Group of Governmental Experts to actively support and promote the Register as one of its primary missions and to address as a priority the human and financial resource challenges faced by the secretariat (A/68/140). The new website for the Register (www.unroca.org/) and the new interface for the online reporting tool (https://www.unroca.org/reporting/login) were particularly welcomed by the Group. The Register is now overseen by a senior political affairs officer (P-5) in the Office for Disarmament Affairs. This position is judged to be commensurate with the level of responsibility that should be associated with the instrument and to reflect the importance attributed to it by Member States (see A/68/140, para. 75). Consideration was also given to the need for one full-time support staff member at the General Service level to assist in the maintenance of the Register's database, management of reports and provision of technical support to national points of contact. The Group stressed the need for the Secretariat to actively encourage Member States to report to the Register, including "nil" returns, and to ensure that

information provided by Member States is made available and accessible in a timely manner. Given the limited resources available to the Secretariat for travel and participation in regional meetings of relevance to the Register, experts considered how the United Nations regional centres for peace and disarmament could promote transparency in armaments and regularly engage with Register national points of contact as well as relevant officials in ministries of defence and security agencies to promote understanding of the objectives of the Register and participation in it.

37. The Group considered a variety of measures that the Secretariat could undertake to raise awareness of the Register, in cooperation with Member States.

K. Reporting methods

38. The Secretariat developed an online reporting tool for the electronic filing of reports to the Register, in response to the recommendations of the 2003 and 2006 Groups of Governmental Experts (A/58/274, para. 114 (f) and A/61/261, para. 126 (n)). Since the online reporting tool was launched in May 2012, 46 Member States have used it to prepare and submit their reports online. The Secretariat has provided informal briefing sessions on the electronic filing of reports to the Register on the margins of the meetings of the First Committee of the General Assembly. A new version of the online reporting tool was presented to the Group in April 2016. As with the previous version, information provided via the online reporting tool is automatically entered into the Register database. It is currently only available in English. Experts were invited to test the online reporting tool between the first and second sessions of the 2016 Group and to provide their views on ease of use and recommendations for further development to the Secretariat.

39. In connection with the decline in reporting to the Register, the Group discussed technical challenges for reporting to the Register at the national level, in particular the request to provide information on actual transfers to the Register. Experts shared national experiences on the different sources of information that are utilized for compiling a national submission to the Register, such as customs, security forces and the arms industry. Experts noted that some Member States reporting to the Register provide information on authorizations (i.e. arms export licences) and not actual transfers. The Group considered providing clarification on the potential sources of information that might be utilized to prepare an annual submission to the Register to increase participation, and how to best provide national points of contact with such guidance.

40. The Group paid particular attention to the practical ways in which the Secretariat and Member States could provide support and guidance for national points of contact to provide information to the Register and also access information. The Group considered a range of options including: (a) updating the information booklet on the United Nations Register of Conventional Arms to reflect developments with regard to the Register since 2007, in particular the online reporting tool; (b) preparing guidance on the role and responsibilities of national points of contact; (c) providing good practice guidance for a national system to prepare a Register submission; and (d) developing a mechanism for matching offers and requests for assistance in filing reports to the Register, including a roster of experts that could provide guidance on methods for data collection and reporting to the Register.

III. Further development of the Register

A. Maintaining the relevance and universality of the Register

41. The Group considered that one of its main tasks was to propose measures to reinvigorate the Register, at a time when the need for confidence-building measures remained high, drawing upon the deliberations and proposals of previous Groups of Governmental

Experts. In that regard, the Group focused on two key issues to maintain the relevance and universality of the Register in connection with its further development: (a) to identify the reasons for declining reporting levels and consider measures to address the decline; and (b) to amend the scope of the Register to reflect the increase in transparency in international arms transfers and developments in conventional arms, and assess the potential impact of such changes on relevance and universality.

42.   In order to better understand and address the decline in reporting, the Group considered the following issues: (a) fact-finding on the reasons for the decline in reporting; (b) raising awareness of the Register, in particular its purpose and utility for building confidence and trust between Member States; (c) measures to support national reporting to the Register; and (d) the role of the Secretariat in the operation and maintenance of the Register.

43.   The Group reviewed a number of proposals for studying the decline in reporting, including: (a) comparing participation in, and the experience of, other United Nations, international and regional reporting mechanisms with the Register; (b) examining the impact and lessons learned of the 10 regional workshops to promote the Register undertaken in Africa (five workshops), Asia and the Pacific (four workshops) and the Americas (one workshop) during the period 2001-2006 and in 2009; and (c) distributing a questionnaire to Member States to gather information on their process for compiling reports, national point of contact, use of the resources offered by the Office for Disarmament Affairs and views on expanding the Register's scope.

44.   The Group considered a number of proposals for raising awareness of the Register, including items contained in the illustrative list of measures to promote reporting to the Register contained in the report of the 2013 Group of Governmental Experts (A/68/140). In particular, the Group noted that the twenty-fifth anniversary of the adoption of General Assembly resolution 46/36 L, which established the Register, merited commemoration through a special event promoting participation in the Register. The Group also encouraged greater interaction between the national points of contact and the Secretariat and also among national points of contact. To facilitate such exchanges, experts proposed the creation of a newsletter and/or the development of a restricted access notice-board on the Register website.

45.   The Group reviewed several methods to support the work of national points of contact, permanent missions to the United Nations in New York and national ministries or agencies responsible for collecting and collating the information to be included in a submission to the Register. Available tools to help with identification of weapons and capacity-building were also discussed. The Group examined a proposal for the development of a guidance note on the roles and responsibilities of the national point of contact, which could be included in an updated version of the information booklet on the United Nations Register of Conventional Arms. The Group discussed current reporting practices, noting that some Member States submitted information on authorizations of exports and imports of conventional arms to the Register.

46.   The Group noted the Secretariat's limited resources and its willingness to explore synergies with other international and regional instruments to facilitate participation in the Register. It noted that United Nations regional centres for peace and disarmament and regional organizations had an important role to play in promoting transparency in international arms transfers. The Group also emphasized ways in which Member States could work with the Office for Disarmament Affairs to deliver the proposals and initiatives they had discussed to achieve universality. In that regard, Member States could contribute to a roster of experts, or share with other Member States through the Office for Disarmament Affairs information about capacity-building and training programmes that could facilitate the participation of Member States in the Register.

47.   The Group continued the discussions of previous Groups of Governmental Experts on the potential effect on the relevance and universality of the Register of amending the Register's scope to include small arms and light weapons and items that could project power, act as force multipliers or provide substantial combat support. In addition, the Group discussed the potential implications of developments in automated versions of conventional arms for the Register. The Group also considered whether facilitating the provision of background information on national holdings and on procurement through national production would positively affect participation in the Register.

48.   Noting that the first annual reports on exports and imports of eight categories of conventional arms were provided to the secretariat of the Arms Trade Treaty by 31 May 2016, the Group discussed the potential impact of that development on the continuing operation of the Register. The Group noted that the Register and the Arms Trade Treaty served different functions and had different memberships, but also that annual reports on imports and exports of conventional arms by States parties to the Arms Trade Treaty might contain the same information as submitted to the Register, including on international transfers of small arms and light weapons. The Group expressed its firm conviction that the Register needed to continue to play its role as the only global voluntary transparency and confidence-building measure in international conventional arms transfers.

49.   The Group paid particular attention to initiatives to support national reporting processes as a means of increasing participation. In order to increase reporting by Member States that do not import or export conventional arms covered by the categories of the Register, the Group debated the appropriateness of allowing such Member States to submit a rolling "nil" return for up to three years. This would mean that a Member State declares that it is submitting a "nil" return to cover up to three years of future reporting because it has no plans to import or export conventional arms covered by the seven categories of the Register during the declared period. The Secretariat would send a note verbale to the Member State each year to enquire if an update is necessary, but would utilize the rolling "nil" return for the period indicated by the Member State when recording that Member State's participation in the Register.

B.   Categories covered by the Register

50.   The Group recognized that its mandate included considering proposals for amending the description of existing categories to ensure that the Register remained relevant for the security concerns of Member States, as well as reflecting developments in other multilateral transparency regimes, technological advances and the nature of contemporary conflict and warfare.

Category I
Battle tanks

51.   The Group considered a proposal for removing the weight limit of 16.5 metric tons from the description of battle tanks. The Group noted that the current description for category II, Armoured combat vehicles, covered tanks that weigh less than 16.5 metric tons.

Category II
Armoured combat vehicles

52.   The Group examined a proposal to expand the scope of category II, Armoured combat vehicles, by including the following force multiplier and force projection items in two additional subcategories:

- equipped for specialized reconnaissance, command and control of troops or electronic warfare;
- armoured recovery vehicles, tank transporters and amphibious and deep-water fording vehicles, including armoured bridge-launching vehicles.

Category III
Large-calibre artillery systems

53. The Group reviewed proposals to lower the calibre threshold of category III to 35 mm or 50 mm and rename the category "Artillery systems". The deliberations noted that changes to this category should take into account the intrinsic link to the issue of the inclusion of small arms and light weapons as a new category, as well as the effect that changes in the category's threshold would have on its focus on "indirect fire" weapons.

Category IV
Combat aircraft

54. The Group reviewed a proposal to expand the description of category IV to cover aircraft that contribute force multiplier effects or force projection capabilities, as follows:

Fixed-wing or variable geometry wing aircraft that are designed, equipped or modified to perform reconnaissance, command and control of troops, specialized electronic warfare and refuelling or airdrop missions.

55. The Group reviewed several options to clarify the status of unmanned aerial vehicles in category IV, Combat aircraft, based on the description contained in paragraph 45 of the report of the 2013 Group of Governmental Experts (A/68/140).

Category V
Attack helicopters

56. The Group reviewed a proposal to expand the description to cover helicopters that contribute force multiplier effects or force projection capabilities, as follows:

Rotary-wing aircraft that are designed, equipped or modified to perform specialized reconnaissance, target acquisition, communications, command and control of troops, electronic warfare, mine-laying missions or troop transport tasks.

57. The Group reviewed several options to clarify the status of rotary-wing unmanned aerial vehicles in category V, Attack helicopters, based on the description contained in paragraph 46 of the report of the 2013 Group of Governmental Experts. The Group's deliberations took into account the proposal to amend the heading and description of category IV, as well as the limited evidence of actual transfers of rotary-wing unmanned combat aerial vehicles to date and developments in the relevant technologies. In particular, the Group considered a proposal to amend both the heading and the description of category V as follows:

Category V
Attack helicopters and rotary-wing unmanned combat aerial vehicles

Includes rotary-wing aerial vehicles as defined below: (a) Manned rotary-wing aircraft, designed, equipped or modified to engage targets by employing guided or unguided anti-armour, air-to-surface, air-to-subsurface or air-to-air weapons and equipped with an integrated fire control and aiming system for these weapons, including versions of these aircraft that perform specialized reconnaissance or electronic warfare missions; (b) Unmanned rotary-wing aircraft, designed, equipped or modified to engage targets by employing guided or unguided anti-armour, air-to-surface, air-to-subsurface or air-to-air weapons and equipped with an integrated fire control and aiming system for these weapons.

Category VI
Warships

58.   The Group reviewed a proposal for amending category VI, Warships, to lower the threshold for the minimum standard displacement of vessels or submarines to 150 metric tons. The Group also examined proposals to lower or remove the range threshold for missiles and torpedoes.

Category VII
Missiles and missile launchers

59.   The Group reviewed proposals to lower or remove the range threshold for missiles and to include ground-to-air missiles and missile launchers.

C.   Expansion of the scope of the Register

60.   A rich and detailed discussion took place when the Group reviewed the long-standing proposal to establish a new main category for small arms and light weapons in the Register.

61.   The Group reviewed the level of reporting of background information on international transfers of small arms and light weapons in accordance with the recommendations of the 2003, 2006, 2009 and 2013 Groups of Governmental Experts, as well as potential adjustments to the Register's scope. Key areas of the debate included the following:

(a)   It was noted that both licit and illicit small arms and light weapon transfers to State security forces and non-state actors can contribute to excessive and destabilizing accumulations, which could have a negative effect on levels of security, stability and armed violence in various regions of the world. The realities of conflict in the twenty-first century were such that efforts to control small arms and light weapons were now a high-priority issue for the international community;

(b)   In that context, increased transparency was an important complement to other efforts being undertaken. The Register covered transfers of conventional arms to Member States, but it was recognized that those transfers could be subject to diversion to the illicit trade. Transparency in the licit transfer of small arms and light weapons was therefore necessary;

(c)   Given the relevance of diverted small arms and light weapons as a security threat, especially to Member States in the African and the Latin American and the Caribbean regions, the Group discussed whether adding them to the existing categories of conventional arms could be both appropriate and conducive to increased reporting. The view was noted that existing reporting mechanisms already included small arms and light weapons as a category, which left the Register lagging behind;

(d)   On the other hand, it was noted that the limited response to the requests of the Secretary-General in 2009 and 2013 for Member States to submit their views on the implications of creating a new category for reporting small arms and light weapons to the Register did not provide sufficient information to inform the Group's deliberations on this issue. Therefore, the Group considered whether the questionnaire being prepared by the Group should also solicit the views of Member States on the issue. The Group discussed whether it might be better to wait for the results of the questionnaire before committing to any change to the current structure of the Register. It was also noted that the topic of small arms and light weapons had been discussed in successive Groups of Governmental Experts for 16 years, and the view was stated that repeated rounds of outreach had already confirmed the relevance of small arms and light weapons as an additional reporting category;

(e) The Group discussed the possibility that security concerns related to small arms and light weapons could actually lead some Member States not to report their transfers to the Register. It was noted that there were security concerns related to other categories in the Register, which sometimes led Member States to submit incomplete returns. This was acceptable in the light of the voluntary nature of reporting to the Register. From a confidence-building perspective, incomplete reports, like "nil" returns, were of greater value than the absence of reporting. At the same time, it was noted that a template for providing additional information on international transfers of small arms and light weapons had already been introduced, which assisted Member States in reporting such transactions to the Register;

(f) The view was noted that caution should be exercised in modifying the structure of the Register, in particular additions to the existing seven categories. Those seven categories had long been used as a point of reference for other purposes. In that context, small arms and light weapons were different in that they had greater relevance for civil wars, internal conflicts and armed violence. It was noted that the definitions of the Register's categories had been employed by the Security Council in arms embargoes in only two instances. That kind of use of the Register's categories was in principle flexible; one, several or all categories could be employed depending on the situation. The view was noted that the underlying security concerns of small arms and light weapons were on a par with concerns related to the other seven categories. The question of labelling or grouping should therefore be considered of secondary importance;

(g) The view was noted that the current seven categories of the Register were composed of weapons indispensable to offensive operations. The utility of this concept would be jeopardized by the addition of small arms and light weapons. In that light, a seven plus one formula (the seven existing categories of the Register, plus small arms and light weapons) was more appropriate. It was noted that the purpose of the Register was to identify excessive and destabilizing accumulations of conventional arms and not to focus on the characteristics of any particular weapons system;

(h) It was also noted that the inclusion of small arms and light weapons among the existing categories would reduce the ability of Member States to provide "nil" returns and could thus represent an increase in the burden of reporting for those States. It was necessary to weigh that factor against the increased incentive for reporting that experts felt was associated with an increased relevance of the Register.

62. The Group noted that the Register did not currently cover all the ways in which Member States could acquire excessive and destabilizing accumulations of conventional arms. That was because Member States were "requested" to provide information on imports, but were only "invited" to provide background information on procurement through national production. That led to a situation in which Member States that procured conventional arms from their national production did not have to provide the same degree of transparency on their acquisitions as those Member States that are dependent on imports of conventional arms. The Group examined a proposal to request Member States to provide information on procurement through national production to the Register on the same basis as for international transfers.

63. The Group noted that Member States providing background information on procurement through national production did so in a variety of formats. The Group considered whether an optional reporting form for additional background information on military holdings could be of benefit for States by providing a structure for such reporting. It noted that the online reporting tool provided a de facto reporting form for the provision of background information on procurement through national production. The Group identified a need for a technical adjustment

to the online reporting tool to enable the uploading of such background information in national reporting formats. Conversely, the Group considered the precedent of the standardized reporting template for background information on international transfers of small arms and light weapons to enable structured reporting and underlined the desirability for all Member States to have access to the de facto reporting form in all the official languages of the United Nations for offline reporting.

64. The Group discussed the provision of background information on military holdings for the purpose of assisting in the identification of excessive and destabilizing accumulations of conventional weapons and for confidence-building purposes. Experts recognized the security sensitivities that that information entailed for some Member States. The Group considered whether an optional reporting form for additional background information on military holdings could be of benefit for States by providing a structure for such reporting. It noted that the online reporting tool provided a de facto reporting form for the provision of background information on military holdings. The Group identified a need for a technical adjustment to the online reporting tool to enable the uploading of background information on military holdings in national reporting formats. Conversely, the Group considered the precedent of the standardized reporting template for background information on international transfers of small arms and light weapons to enable structured reporting and underlined the desirability for all Member States to have access to the de facto reporting form in all United Nations official languages for offline reporting.

D. Review of the Register

65. The Group emphasized the importance of conducting periodic reviews of the Register to enhance its operation and consider its further development. That was necessary to achieve universal participation and ensure the Register's relevance for Member States as a confidence-building measure in the light of changing security dynamics, in particular with regard to technological developments in conventional arms.

E. Relationship between the Register and other relevant international and regional instruments

66. The Group noted that the Register had served as an inspiration and reference point for international and regional initiatives and instruments to strengthen control over international transfers of conventional arms, thereby enhancing transparency in armaments and building confidence between States. The Group stressed that important lessons could be learned from the experience of 25 years of reporting to the Register, but that lessons could also be learned from reporting to other international and regional instruments on international transfers of conventional arms. The Group discussed a concern that Member States might give a higher priority to reporting to other instruments rather than the Register, in particular instruments where reporting was a legally binding obligation, or where the instrument was regarded as more relevant for the security interests and concerns of the Member State. Therefore, the Group emphasized the importance of encouraging Member States to identify synergies between different reporting instruments, and considered recommendations to enhance reporting to the Register that could indirectly benefit other reporting as well.

IV. Conclusions and recommendations

A. Conclusions

67. The Group concluded that the twenty-fifth anniversary of the establishment of the Register was an ideal opportunity for raising awareness of the Register's achievements and

its role in increasing transparency in international arms transfers. The Register served as an important point of reference and inspiration for regional and international confidence-building mechanisms, arms control and transfer control instruments. The Group agreed that the anniversary represented an important opportunity to promote the Register's continued role as the only global instrument for transparency in international arms transfers.

68. The Group expressed serious concern at the decline in reporting to the Register since 2008, in particular the lowest level of reporting to the Register in 2012. Experts proposed a number of measures addressed to the Secretariat and Member States to promote the Register and enable greater participation. The Group concluded that a concerted effort was needed to better understand the reasons for the decline in participation in the Register, which could help to inform further, targeted measures to reverse the decline. The Group considered methods to collect the views of as many Member States as possible on the operation and development of the Register.

69. The Group recognized that the substantial decline in the number of Member States submitting "nil" returns had significantly contributed to the overall decline in participation in the Register since 2008. A "nil" return was as important as a submission on a Member State's imports and exports of conventional arms for building trust and confidence among Member States. The Group noted that there was a simplified form for filing a nil "return" using the online reporting tool or in hard copy. The Group discussed how to facilitate an increase in the level of participation by Member States that regularly filed a "nil" return during the early 2000s, but which had not participated regularly in the Register during the years 2012-2015. In particular, the Group considered the option of permitting the submission of a rolling "nil" return. That approach was intended for use by Member States that did not have plans to procure items covered by the Register's categories for several years.

70. The Group considered a number of measures to encourage the development and maintenance of national systems to support regular participation in the Register. The Group reviewed initiatives by regional organizations and multilateral export control regimes to develop guidelines for establishing and maintaining effective national reporting systems. Experts considered updating the information booklet on the United Nations Register of Conventional Arms to include guidance to ensure an effective national reporting system. The Group also considered the various methods for sharing experience in developing national reporting systems and supporting capacity-building. In addition to calling upon Member States to assist, upon request, with capacity-building and training to enable Member States to participate in the Register, the Group considered the potential contributions of the Office for Disarmament Affairs, its regional centres and other regional and international organizations, as well as opportunities for online training and capacity-building, including via the Register's website.

71. The Group recognized the challenges that some Member States faced in reporting on actual exports and imports of conventional arms. In some cases, national systems recorded data and information only on authorizations of exports and imports of conventional arms. The Group noted that such Member States reported on authorizations to the Register in order to contribute to confidence-building. When that option was exercised, those Member States should indicate in their national submission that their data and information referred to authorizations for exports and imports of conventional arms.

72. The Group stressed the importance of Member States designating a national point of contact for the Register. The Group encouraged Member States to provide the Secretariat with details of their national point of contact. If the details of their national point of contact changed, then the Member State should provide its new information to the Secretariat in a timely manner. The Secretariat should maintain and update the list of national points of contact

to ensure it could communicate regularly and directly with the national points of contact on matters pertaining to the Register, in particular updates on data and information provided by Member States to the Register, new developments with regard to the online reporting tool and guidelines, assistance opportunities for training and capacity-building for national points of contact, and reporting deadline reminders. The list of national points of contact should be made available to Member States to enable communication between national points of contact to allow corroboration and clarification of data submitted, as well as for sharing information on national practices relating to reporting and participation in the Register. The Group considered the development of guidance with regard to the role, tasks and responsibility of national points of contact, and its inclusion in an updated version of the information booklet on the United Nations Register of Conventional Arms. It also discussed the option of including a restricted access area on the Register website to facilitate exchanges between national points of contact.

73.　The Group noted that an increasing number of Member States had committed to provide data and information on an annual basis on their international transfers of conventional arms to regional and international instruments, in addition to the Register. The Group noted that similarities in content and format existed that enabled Members States to utilize the data and other information contained in their annual submissions on arms exports and imports to the Register for reporting forms used by other instruments, and vice versa. The Group encouraged Member States and the Secretariat to explore opportunities to reduce the reporting burden for such Member States. In particular, the Group welcomed collaboration between the Register secretariat and the secretariats for relevant regional and international instruments to promote participation in the Register and support efforts by Member States to report on their international transfers of conventional arms.

74.　The Group noted that the proposals for adjustments to the existing seven categories of the Register, reflected in paragraphs 51-54 and 56-59 above, should be further reviewed by the next Group of Governmental Experts.

75.　The Group discussed the relationship between existing categories and a possible new category in the Register for reporting small arms and light weapons. The Group noted the view that the diversion of licit transfers of small arms and light weapons posed a threat to security and that transparency of licit transfers of small arms and light weapons could contribute to building confidence and trust between Member States. The Group also noted the view that reporting on international transfers of small arms and light weapons could increase the reporting burden for some Member States and could discourage some Member States from reporting to the Register. Taking into account calls to include small arms and light weapons as a new category in the Register, and at the same time considering the implications of such a step for the existing structure of the Register, the Group discussed the possibility of utilizing the seven plus one formula for a trial period to inform the deliberations of the next Group of Governmental Experts on the possible establishment of a new category for small arms and light weapons in the Register. The Group viewed the seven plus one formula as the reporting of international transfers of small arms and light weapons by Member States in parallel with the seven categories of the Register, using the standardized reporting form for international transfers of small arms and light weapons. Small arms and light weapons would not be represented as an eighth category on the standardized reporting form used for the seven existing categories. The Group recognized that such a trial use of the seven plus one formula, as well as the results of the proposed questionnaire, could greatly benefit the deliberations of the next Group of Governmental Experts on the possible inclusion in the Register of a new category for reporting small arms and light weapons.

76. The Group concluded that the results of the triennial review of the Register should seek to increase participation in the Register by different means, including by strengthening the scope of the Register to take into account technological developments with regard to conventional arms, the changing dynamics of the international arms trade and the nature of contemporary conflict. Mindful of the approach promoted by the 2006 Group of Governmental Experts (see A/61/261) with regard to the development of a standardized reporting form for additional background information on international transfers of small arms and light weapons, the Group considered proposals for including procurement through national production on the same basis as international transfers. The Group noted that standardized reporting forms could be of particular use for those Member States that utilized the online reporting tool for electronic filing of their annual submissions.

77. The Group reaffirmed the importance of regular and timely reporting to the Register, including "nil" returns. The Group noted that it was useful to receive a confirmation of receipt when a report had been submitted via the online reporting tool. The Group assessed the benefits of translating the online reporting tool for the electronic filing of submissions into all official languages of the United Nations as soon as possible.

78. The Group expressed its satisfaction at the introduction of the updated online reporting tool for the electronic filing of submissions and the overhaul of the Register's website and online database. The Group stressed the importance of providing timely and easily accessible access to data and information provided by Member States. It therefore encouraged the Secretariat to update the online Register database when individual Member States provided their annual submission to the Secretariat. The Group also encouraged the Secretariat to promote the new online database and consider a regular press release after the 31 May deadline. Finally, the Group encouraged the Secretariat and other United Nations agencies to examine how information provided by Member States to the Register could be utilized for United Nations initiatives for peace, international security and conflict-prevention.

79. The Group reaffirmed the conclusions of previous Groups of Governmental Experts that the Conventional Arms Branch of the Office for Disarmament Affairs should actively support and promote the Register as one of its primary missions. The Group welcomed the strengthening of the Register secretariat to enable it to fulfil its mandated responsibilities in that regard. It expressed its view that the Office for Disarmament Affairs should be provided with adequate financial resources and personnel to strengthen the secretariat's role in raising awareness of the Register and promoting participation. The Group also encouraged Member States to provide voluntary contributions to the secretariat to support those efforts.

80. The Group stressed the importance of regular reviews of the continuing operation of the Register and its further development. The Group supported the calls of the 2009 and 2013 Groups of Governmental Experts for the regular review of the Register to be undertaken by Groups of Governmental Experts given ample time to conduct their review and representing different perspectives on transparency in armaments on the basis of equitable geographical representation.

B. Recommendations

81. Following extensive discussion of proposals for adjustments to the categories of the Register, the Group recommends that the heading for category IV be amended as shown below and that the following definition be used for reporting to the Register items covered by category IV (see annex I):

Category IV
Combat aircraft and unmanned combat aerial vehicles

Includes fixed-wing or variable-geometry wing aerial vehicles as defined below:

(a) Manned fixed-wing or variable-geometry wing aircraft, designed, equipped or modified to engage targets by employing guided missiles, unguided rockets, bombs, guns, cannons or other weapons of destruction, including versions of these aircraft which perform specialized electronic warfare, suppression of air defence or reconnaissance missions;

(b) Unmanned fixed-wing or variable-geometry wing aircraft, designed, equipped or modified to engage targets by employing guided missiles, unguided rockets, bombs, guns, cannons or other weapons of destruction.

The terms "combat aircraft" and "unmanned combat aerial vehicles" do not include primary trainer aircraft, unless designed, equipped or modified as described above.

82. The Group recommends that the next Group of Governmental Experts further consider the proposal contained in paragraph 57 above to amend the heading and definition for category V, Attack helicopters, paying particular attention to actual transfers of, and developments in relevant technologies of, rotary-wing unmanned combat aerial vehicles. Pending the recommendation of a future Group of Governmental Experts to amend the heading and definition of category V, those Member States providing information on international transfers of rotary-wing unmanned combat aerial vehicles, are encouraged to utilize the comments column of the reporting form to identify these systems (see annex II).

83. The Group recommends that the Secretary-General appeal to Member States in a position to do so to provide information on international transfers of small arms and light weapons using the standardized reporting form for international transfers of small arms and light weapons (see annex III). The Group recommends that the seven plus one formula, as described in paragraph 75 above, be utilized on a trial basis for the period leading up to the deliberations of the next Group of Governmental Experts, and that the response to this trial use inform the deliberations of the next Group of Governmental Experts on whether to include small arms and light weapons as a new category in the Register. These deliberations should also take into account the results of the recommended questionnaire and other information regarding this issue.

84. The Group recommends that the Secretary-General continue to invite Member States in a position to do so to provide data and information on procurement through national production to the Register as part of their additional background information. Member States providing such information are invited to use the de facto reporting form on procurement through national production. This does not preclude Member States from using any other method of reporting they deem appropriate.

85. The Group recommends that the Secretary-General continue to invite Member States in a position to do so to provide data and information on military holdings to the Register as part of their additional background information. Member States providing such information are invited to use the de facto reporting form on military holdings. This does not preclude Member States from using any other method of reporting they deem appropriate.

86. To gain a better understanding of national reporting systems and challenges that Member States might face in reporting to the Register, the Group recommends that the Office for Disarmament Affairs distribute the questionnaire attached to the present report as annex V, which could aid the Secretariat's future work and that of future Groups of Governmental Experts. The questionnaire seeks the views of Member States on the continuing operation of the Register and its further development, including on whether the absence of small arms and

light weapons as a main category in the Register has limited its relevance and directly affected decisions on participation.

87.   The Group recommends that the Secretariat update and reissue the information booklet on the United Nations Register of Conventional Arms. This information booklet should be made easily accessible on the Register website and be provided in all official languages of the United Nations. The Group recommends that the updated Guidelines should also include: (a) guidance on establishing and maintaining effective national reporting systems; and (b) guidance with regard to the role, tasks and responsibility of national points of contact (see annex IV).

88.   The Group recommends that Member States report by the 31 May deadline in order to facilitate early compilation and dissemination of data and information provided in the annual submissions of Member States. The Group also recommends that Member States utilize the updated online reporting tool for the electronic filing of reports. The Group recommends that the Secretariat should circulate to Member States the reporting forms, category descriptions and guidance on using the online reporting tool for the electronic filing of submissions, under cover of a note verbale to permanent missions to the United Nations in New York, as well as copies to national points of contact, at the beginning of each year. The Secretariat should also send subsequent reminders to permanent missions to the United Nations in New York and to national points of contact to help to facilitate submissions.

89.   To facilitate higher levels of participation, the Group recommends that Member States be provided with the opportunity to submit a "nil" return valid for a maximum of three years. The Secretariat should continue to send an annual request to participate in the Register to such Member States, but these Member States would only have to respond if imports or exports of conventional arms have taken place during the reporting period.

90.   The Group recommends that the translation of the online reporting tool into all official languages of the United Nations be a priority for the continuing operation of the Register. The Group recognizes that additional resources will need to be provided to the Secretariat in order to complete the tasks described in paragraphs 90-92 of the present report and recommends that Member States consider providing financial support to the Secretariat to fulfil these recommendations.

91.   The Group recommends that the online Register database be updated as soon as possible after receipt of new data and information from Member States. In addition, the new Register website and database merits a press release to draw attention to this new resource, ideally after it has been updated with information provided by Member States regarding transfers for the 2015 calendar year. The Register website should serve as the main repository for all basic data and information relevant to the Register and should be available in all official languages of the United Nations.

92.   To mark the occasion of the twenty-fifth anniversary of the establishment of the Register, an event should be organized on the margins of the First Committee at the seventy-first session of the General Assembly. This event could also be used to promote the new Register website and database and the report of the 2016 Group of Governmental Experts. The anniversary should also be reflected in the General Assembly resolution on transparency in armaments to be adopted at its seventy-first session. Other opportunities to promote the Register should also be examined, including through the regional centres of the Office for Disarmament Affairs.

93.   In order to facilitate universal participation and continued development of the Register, the Group recommends convening a Group of Governmental Experts in 2019 to review

the operation of the Register and consider its further development. The Group should consist of at least 20 experts representing the diverse perspectives on transparency in armaments of Member States on the basis of equitable geographical representation.

94.   The Group recommends that future reviews of the continuing operation and further development of the Register consider the conclusions and recommendations of the present report, as well as those contained in the reports of previous Groups of Governmental Experts, including the illustrative list of measures to promote reporting to the Register contained in the report of the 2013 Group of Governmental Experts (A/68/140, annex).

Annex I

Categories of equipment and their definitions

Category I
Battle tanks

Tracked or wheeled self-propelled armoured fighting vehicles with high cross-country mobility and a high-level of self-protection, weighing at least 16.5 metric tons unladen weight, with a high muzzle velocity direct fire main gun of at least 75 millimetres calibre.

Category II
Armoured combat vehicles

Tracked, semi-tracked or wheeled self-propelled vehicles, with armoured protection and cross-country capability, either: (a) designed and equipped to transport a squad of four or more infantrymen; or (b) armed with an integral or organic weapon of at least 12.5 millimetres calibre or a missile launcher.

Category III
Large-calibre artillery systems

Guns, howitzers, artillery pieces, combining the characteristics of a gun or a howitzer, mortars or multiple-launch rocket systems, capable of engaging surface targets by delivering primarily indirect fire, with a calibre of 75 millimetres and above.

Category IV
Combat aircraft and unmanned combat aerial vehicles

Includes fixed-wing or variable-geometry wing aerial vehicles as defined below:

(a) Manned fixed-wing or variable-geometry wing aircraft, designed, equipped or modified to engage targets by employing guided missiles, unguided rockets, bombs, guns, cannons or other weapons of destruction, including versions of these aircraft which perform specialized electronic warfare, suppression of air defence or reconnaissance missions;

(b) Unmanned fixed-wing or variable-geometry wing aircraft, designed, equipped or modified to engage targets by employing guided missiles, unguided rockets, bombs, guns, cannons or other weapons of destruction;

The terms "combat aircraft" and "unmanned combat aerial vehicles" do not include primary trainer aircraft, unless designed, equipped or modified as described above.

Category V
Attack helicopters

Rotary-wing aircraft designed, equipped or modified to engage targets by employing guided or unguided anti-armour, air-to-surface, air-to-subsurface or air-to-air weapons and equipped with an integrated fire control and aiming system for these weapons, including versions of these aircraft which perform specialized reconnaissance or electronic warfare missions.

Category VI
Warships

Vessels or submarines armed and equipped for military use with a standard displacement of 500 metric tons or above, and those with a standard displacement of less than 500 metric tons, equipped for launching missiles with a range of at least 25 kilometres or torpedoes with similar range.

Category VII
Missiles and missile launchers

(a)   Guided or unguided rockets, ballistic or cruise missiles capable of delivering a warhead or weapon of destruction to a range of at least 25 kilometres, and means designed or modified specifically for launching such missiles or rockets, if not covered by categories I through VI. For the purpose of the Register, this subcategory includes remotely piloted vehicles with the characteristics for missiles as defined above but does not include ground-to-air missiles;

(b)   Man-portable air-defence systems.

Annex II

Standardized form for reporting international transfers of conventional arms

Exports[a]

Report of international conventional arms transfers
(according to General Assembly resolutions 46/36 L and 58/54)

Reporting country: _____

National point of contact: _____

(Organization, Division/Section, telephone, fax, e-mail) (FOR GOVERNMENTAL USE ONLY)

Calendar year: _____

A	B	C	D[b]	E[b]	Remarks[c]	
Category (I-VII)	Final importer State(s)	Number of items	State of origin (if not exporter)	Intermediate location (if any)	Description of item	Comments on the transfer
I. Battle tanks						
II. Armoured combat vehicles						
III. Large-calibre artillery systems						
IV. Combat aircraft and unmanned combat aerial vehicles						
(a) Combat aircraft						
(b) Unmanned combat aerial vehicles						
V. Attack helicopters[d]						
VI. Warships						
VII. Missiles and missile launchers[e]						
(a) Missiles and missile launchers						
(b) Man-portable air-defence systems						

National criteria on transfers:

[a b c d e] See explanatory notes.

The nature of information provided should be indicated in accordance with explanatory notes f and g.

Standardized form for reporting international transfers of conventional arms

Imports[a]

Report of international conventional arms transfers
(according to General Assembly resolutions 46/36 L and 58/54)

Reporting country: _____

National point of contact: _____

(Organization, Division/Section, telephone, fax, e-mail) (FOR GOVERNMENTAL USE ONLY)

Calendar year: _____

A	*B*	*C*	*D[b]*	*E[b]*	*Remarks[c]*	
Category (I–VII)	*Final importer State(s)*	*Number of items*	*State of origin (if not exporter)*	*Intermediate location (if any)*	*Description of item*	*Comments on the transfer*
I. Battle tanks						
II. Armoured combat vehicles						
III. Large-calibre artillery systems						
IV. Combat aircraft and unmanned combat aerial vehicles						
(a) Combat aircraft						
(b) Unmanned combat aerial vehicles						
V. Attack helicopters[d]						
VI. Warships						
VII. Missiles and missile launchers[e]						
(a) Missiles and missile launchers						
(b) Man-portable air-defence systems						

National criteria on transfers:
[a b c d e] See explanatory notes.

The nature of information provided should be indicated in accordance with explanatory notes f and g.

Explanatory notes

(a) Member States that do not have anything to report should file a "nil" report clearly stating that no exports or imports have taken place in any of the categories during the reporting period.

(b) International arms transfers involve, in addition to the physical movement of equipment into or from national territory, the transfer of title to and control over the equipment. Member States are invited to provide with their return a concise explanation of national criteria used to determine when an arms transfer becomes effective (see paragraph 42 of the annex to document A/49/316).

(c) In the "Remarks" column Member States may wish to describe the item transferred by entering the designation, type, model or any other information considered relevant. Member States may also wish to use the "Remarks" column to explain or clarify aspects relevant to the transfer.

(d) The 2016 Group of Governmental Experts recommends that those Member States providing information on international transfers of rotary-wing unmanned combat aerial vehicles utilize the comments column of the reporting form to identify these systems.

(e) Multiple-launch rocket systems are covered by the definition of category III. Rockets qualifying for registration are covered under category VII. Man-portable air-defence systems should be reported if the system is supplied as a complete unit, i.e. the missile and launcher/grip stock form an integral unit. In addition, individual launching mechanisms or grip stocks should also be reported. Individual missiles not supplied with a launching mechanism or grip stock need not be reported.

(f) Check any of the following provided as part of your submission:

		Check
(i)	Annual report on exports of arms	_____
(ii)	Annual report on imports of arms	_____
(iii)	Available background information on military holdings	_____
(iv)	Available background information on procurement through national production	_____
(v)	Available background information on relevant policies and/or national legislation	_____
(vi)	Other (please describe)	_____

(g) When reporting transfers, which of the following criteria, drawn from paragraph 42 of the annex to document A/49/316, were used:

		Check
(i)	Departure of equipment from the exporter's territory	_____
(ii)	Arrival of equipment in the importer's territory	_____
(iii)	Transfer of title	_____
(iv)	Transfer of control	_____
(v)	Other (please provide brief description below)	_____

Annex III

Form for reporting international transfers of small arms and light weapons[a,b] on a trial basis[c]

Exports

Reporting country: _____

National point of contact: _____

(Organization, Division/Section, telephone, fax, e-mail) (FOR GOVERNMENTAL USE ONLY)

Calendar year: _____

A	B	C	D	E	Remarks	
	Final importer State(s)	Number of items	State of origin (if not exporter)	Intermediate location (if any)	Description of item	Comments on the transfer
SMALL ARMS						
1. Revolvers and self-loading pistols						
2. Rifles and carbines						
3. Sub-machine guns						
4. Assault rifles						
5. Light machine guns						
6. Other						
LIGHT WEAPONS						
1. Heavy machine guns						
2. Hand-held under-barrel and mounted grenade launchers						
3. Portable anti-tank guns						
4. Recoilless rifles						
5. Portable anti-tank missile launchers and rocket systems						
6. Mortars of calibres less than 75 mm						
7. Other						

National criteria on transfers:

[a] The standardized forms provide options for reporting only aggregate quantities under the generic categories of "Small arms" and "Light weapons" and/or under their respective subcategories. See the information booklet on the United Nations Register of Conventional Arms (www.un.org/disarmament/publications/more/register-conv-arms) for questions and answers regarding the reporting of small arms and light weapons.

[b] The categories provided in the reporting form do not constitute a definition of "Small arms" or "Light weapons".

[c] This form is intended for use for providing information on international transfers of "small arms and light weapons" on a trial basis in accordance with the recommendation contained in paragraph 83 of the 2016 Group of Governmental Expert's report (A/71/259). It is the reporting form for "Information on international transfers of small arms and light weapons" that was adopted by the 2006 Group of Governmental Experts.

Form for reporting international transfers of small arms and light weapons[a,b] on a trial basis[c]

Imports

Reporting country: _____

National point of contact: _____

(Organization, Division/Section, telephone, fax, e-mail) (FOR GOVERNMENTAL USE ONLY)

Calendar year: _____

	A	B	C	D	E	Remarks	
		Final importer State(s)	Number of items	State of origin (if not exporter)	Intermediate location (if any)	Description of item	Comments on the transfer
SMALL ARMS							
1.	Revolvers and self-loading pistols						
2.	Rifles and carbines						
3.	Sub-machine guns						
4.	Assault rifles						
5.	Light machine guns						
6.	Other						
LIGHT WEAPONS							
1.	Heavy machine guns						
2.	Hand-held under-barrel and mounted grenade launchers						
3.	Portable anti-tank guns						
4.	Recoilless rifles						
5.	Portable anti-tank missile launchers and rocket systems						
6.	Mortars of calibres less than 75 mm						
7.	Other						

National criteria on transfers:

[a] The standardized forms provide options for reporting only aggregate quantities under the generic categories of "Small arms" and "Light weapons" and/or under their respective subcategories. See the information booklet on the United Nations Register of Conventional Arms (www.un.org/disarmament/publications/more/register-conv-arms/) for questions and answers regarding the reporting of small arms and light weapons.

[b] The categories provided in the reporting form do not constitute a definition of "Small arms" or "Light weapons".

[c] This form is intended for use for providing information on international transfers of "small arms and light weapons" on a trial basis in accordance with the recommendation contained in paragraph 83 of the 2016 Group of Governmental Expert's report (A/71/259). It is the reporting form for "Information on international transfers of small arms and light weapons" that was adopted by the 2006 Group of Governmental Experts.

Annex IV

Importance of the points of contact in enhancing the value of the United Nations Register of Conventional Arms for Member States

1.   The main role of the point of contact at the national level is to facilitate timely and reliable reporting to the Register. By maintaining effective procedures for collecting and processing data, as well as generating awareness of the benefits of reporting, the point of contact can play a key role in the success of the Register. Close cooperation between the point of contact and the Office for Disarmament Affairs of the Secretariat should therefore be encouraged. Cooperation between points of contact and the Office for Disarmament Affairs could include:

(a)   The Office for Disarmament Affairs regularly updating points of contact on developments regarding reporting modalities, website upgrades and the further development of the framework of the Register;

(b)   The Office for Disarmament Affairs facilitating the participation of points of contact in Group of Governmental Experts meetings as experts or presenters;

(c)   The Office for Disarmament Affairs facilitating networking of points of contact at the regional level;

(d)   Points of contact ensuring that the list of points of contact maintained by the Office for Disarmament Affairs is updated when there are personnel changes;

(e)   Points of contact informing the Office for Disarmament Affairs of the national-level methodology developed for reporting with the purpose of encouraging best practices. The Office for Disarmament Affairs should make such information available to all points of contact;

(f)   Points of contact assisting in the efforts of the Office for Disarmament Affairs to promote good practices in the organization of reporting work.

2.   Empowerment of the points of contact through information-sharing and support may assist them in initiating and managing the inter-agency process and procedures which are necessary for reliable reporting within required deadlines.

3.   The creation of a document setting out national procedures could contribute to the stability of the national reporting process to the Register and other instruments. Such a document could contain, but would not be limited to, the following elements:

(a)   An enumeration of the different types of national reports required to be submitted;

(b)   A clear explanation of the contents and requirements for each type of report, including, for example, the specific categories of items;

(c)   Clear assignment of specific reporting tasks to specific authorities and positions;

(d)   Critical deadlines in the process of preparing reports and a mechanism by which these can be brought to the attention of relevant information providers, for instance through paper or electronic reminders, in order to improve compliance;

(e)   A clearly defined collection process by which information is gathered by licensing/permit officers or other individuals or systems and provided, periodically or on an ongoing basis, to the individual or individuals responsible for preparing and submitting the national reports;

(f)   A coordinated collection process which ensures that when the same information is needed for several reports it is collected only once. This saves time and resources and ensures consistency between reports;

(g) Provision for providing information in national reports as to whether the data submitted is based on actual transfers (exports or imports) or licences issued, if the export or import is temporary, and, if values are reported, what currency or conversion method has been used.

Annex V

Questionnaire on the United Nations Register of Conventional Arms

I am very grateful for your time and cooperation in the completion of this questionnaire. Please enter your answers in the grey boxes, save the file as a word document and forward it to <XXX@un.org>

Details of questionnaire respondent:

Name:

Position:

Department:

Ministry/agency/organization:

Telephone number:

Fax:

E-mail:

Section 1. Process and challenges in compiling national reports for the United Nations Register of Conventional Arms

1. Have you developed a national mechanism for the compilation and submission of your national report for the United Nations Register of Conventional Arms?

   Yes ☐
   No ☐

2. Does your State compile and submit a national report on international transfers of conventional weapons for another international or regional instrument?

   Yes ☐
   No ☐
   If yes, please specify which other instrument(s).

3. Does your State have sufficient resources to compile data for your national report?

   Yes ☐
   No ☐

4. Do you face technical challenges when compiling your data?

   Yes ☐
   No ☐
   If yes, please specify the technical challenges you face.

5. Does your State require technical assistance in compiling your data for the United Nations Register of Conventional Arms?

   Yes ☐
   No ☐
   If yes, could the Secretariat contact you to follow up regarding your assistance needs?
   Yes ☐
   No ☐

Section 2. National reporting authority

1. Has your State appointed a national point of contact?

    Yes ☐
    No ☐

    If yes, please provide information (name and e-mail) of your national point of contact. ▓▓▓▓

    Please also provide information (name and e-mail) of your preferred point of contact at your permanent mission to the Office for Disarmament Affairs in New York. ▓▓▓▓

    If no, please share the reasons for this with the Office for Disarmament Affairs. ▓▓▓▓

2. Has your State provided information to the Office for Disarmament Affairs on your national point of contact?

    Yes ☐
    No ☐

    If no, please provide information (name and e-mail) on your national point of contact. ▓▓▓▓

    Please also provide information (name and e-mail) on your preferred contact in your permanent mission to the United Nations in New York. ▓▓▓▓

3. Please indicate who is responsible for **compiling** your national report for the United Nations Register of Conventional Arms?

    National point of contact ☐
    Permanent mission to the United Nations ☐
    If neither, please specify who is responsible. ▓▓▓▓

4. Please indicate who is responsible for **submitting** the national report for the United Nations Register of Conventional Arms?

    National point of contact ☐
    Permanent mission to the United Nations ☐
    If neither, please specify who is responsible. ▓▓▓▓

Section 3. Availability of online United Nations Register of Conventional Arms resources

1. Are you aware that the Office for Disarmament Affairs website (www.unroca.org/reporting/login) has a standardized reporting form to help when compiling and submitting annual reports?

    Yes ☐
    No ☐

2. Are you aware that the Office for Disarmament Affairs website has an online reporting tool (www.unroca.org/reporting/login) to help when compiling and submitting annual reports?

    Yes ☐
    No ☐

3. Do you know that there are general guidelines on the responsibilities of national points of contact on the website of the United Nations Register of Conventional Arms (https://www.unroca.org)?

    Yes ☐
    No ☐

4. Do you find the new United Nations Register of Conventional Arms website (www.unroca.org) useful for accessing data on international transfers of conventional arms?

    Yes ☐
    No ☐
    If "no", please elaborate. ▒▒▒▒

Section 4. Expanding the scope

1. Does the inclusion on a trial basis of small arms and light weapons in parallel with the existing seven categories of the United Nations Register of Conventional Arms help to increase the relevance of the Register?

    Yes ☐
    No ☐

2. Would you be in favour of the inclusion of small arms and light weapons as a new category of the United Nations Register of Conventional Arms?

    Yes ☐
    No ☐
    Undecided ☐
    If "no" or "undecided", please elaborate. ▒▒▒▒

3. Would you be in favour of reporting any or all of the following on the same basis as international transfers of items covered by the existing seven categories of the United Nations Register of Conventional Arms?

Procurement through national production	Yes ☐	No ☐
Military holdings	Yes ☐	No ☐
Other	Yes ☐	No ☐

    If yes for "other", please specify. ▒▒▒▒

Section 5. Other inputs

1. Will your country submit a report to the United Nations Register of Conventional Arms by 31 May 20XX?

    Yes ☐
    No ☐
    If no, please specify why.

2. Is the United Nations Register of Conventional Arms a relevant instrument for your State?

    Yes ☐
    No ☐
    If no, please specify why.

3. General Assembly resolution XX/XX requests Member States to provide their views on the continuing operation of the Register and its further development. If you would like to provide your views, please use the box below:

Part 3

A/RES/68/43

Resolution adopted by the General Assembly on 5 December 2013

Transparency in armaments

The General Assembly,

Recalling its resolutions 46/36 L of 9 December 1991, 47/52 L of 15 December 1992, 48/75 E of 16 December 1993, 49/75 C of 15 December 1994, 50/70 D of 12 December 1995, 51/45 H of 10 December 1996, 52/38 R of 9 December 1997, 53/77 V of 4 December 1998, 54/54 O of 1 December 1999, 55/33 U of 20 November 2000, 56/24 Q of 29 November 2001, 57/75 of 22 November 2002, 58/54 of 8 December 2003, 60/226 of 23 December 2005, 61/77 of 6 December 2006, 63/69 of 2 December 2008, 64/54 of 2 December 2009 and 66/39 of 2 December 2011, entitled "Transparency in armaments",

Continuing to take the view that an enhanced level of transparency in armaments contributes greatly to confidence-building and security among States and that the establishment of the United Nations Register of Conventional Arms constitutes an important step forward in the promotion of transparency in military matters,

Welcoming the consolidated reports of the Secretary-General on the Register, which include the returns of Member States for 2009,[1] 2010[2] and 2011,[3]

Welcoming also the response of Member States to the request contained in paragraphs 9 and 10 of resolution 46/36 L to provide data on their imports and exports of arms, as well as available background information regarding their military holdings, procurement through national production and relevant policies,

Welcoming further the inclusion by Member States in a position to do so of their transfers of small arms and light weapons in their annual report to the Register as part of their additional background information,

Welcoming the adoption on 2 April 2013 of the Arms Trade Treaty,[4] as well as its signatures and ratifications up to the present date, and the increase in transparency in armaments that will be provided by the Treaty,

Expressing its hope that the Treaty will soon enter into force,

---

[1] A/65/133 and Add.1–5.
[2] A/66/127 and Corr.1 and 2 and Add.1.
[3] A/67/212 and Corr.1 and 2 and Add.1 and 2.
[4] See resolution 67/234 B.

Noting the focused discussions on transparency in armaments that took place in the Conference on Disarmament in 2010, 2011 and 2012,

Expressing its concern with respect to the reduction in reporting to the Register, in particular the low level of reporting to the Register in 2012,

Stressing that the continuing operation of the Register and its further development should be reviewed in order to secure a Register that is capable of attracting the widest possible participation,

1.   *Reaffirms its determination* to ensure the effective operation of the United Nations Register of Conventional Arms, as provided for in paragraphs 7 to 10 of resolution 46/36 L;

2.   *Endorses* the report of the Secretary-General on the continuing operation of the Register and its further development and the recommendations contained in the consensus report of the 2013 group of governmental experts;[5]

3.   *Calls upon* Member States, with a view to achieving universal participation, to provide the Secretary-General, by 31 May annually, with the requested data and information for the Register, including nil reports if appropriate, on the basis of resolutions 46/36 L and 47/52 L, the recommendations contained in paragraph 64 of the 1997 report of the Secretary-General on the continuing operation of the Register and its further development,[6] the recommendations contained in paragraph 94 of the 2000 report of the Secretary-General and the appendices and annexes thereto,[7] the recommendations contained in paragraphs 112 to 114 of the 2003 report of the Secretary-General,[8] the recommendations contained in paragraphs 123 to 127 of the 2006 report of the Secretary-General,[9] the recommendations contained in paragraphs 71 to 75 of the 2009 report of the Secretary-General[10] and the recommendations contained in paragraphs 69 to 76 of the 2013 report of the Secretary-General;[5]

4.   *Invites* Member States in a position to do so, pending further development of the Register, to provide additional information on procurement through national production and military holdings and to make use of the "Remarks" column in the standardized reporting form to provide additional information such as types or models;

5.   *Also invites* Member States in a position to do so to provide additional information on transfers of small arms and light weapons on the basis of the optional standardized reporting form, as adopted by the 2006 group of governmental experts,[11] or by any other methods they deem appropriate;

6.   *Reaffirms* its decision, with a view to further development of the Register, to keep the scope of and participation in the Register under review, and to that end:

(*a*)   Recalls its request to Member States to provide the Secretary-General with their views on the continuing operation of the Register and its further development, including on whether the absence of small arms and light weapons as a main category in the Register has limited its relevance and directly affected decisions on participation, and on transparency measures related to weapons of mass destruction;

(*b*)   Requests the Secretary-General, with the assistance of a group of governmental experts to be convened in 2016, within existing resources, with the broadest possible participation, in line with the recommendation contained in paragraph 76 of the 2013 report of

---

[5]   A/68/140.
[6]   A/52/316 and Corr.2.
[7]   A/55/281.
[8]   A/58/274.
[9]   A/61/261.
[10] A/64/296.
[11] A/61/261, annexes I and II.

the Secretary-General, and on the basis of equitable geographical representation, to prepare a report on the continuing operation and relevance of the Register and its further development, taking into account the work of the Conference on Disarmament, relevant deliberations within the United Nations, the views expressed by Member States and the reports of the Secretary-General on the continuing operation of the Register and its further development, with a view to taking a decision at its seventy-first session;

(*c*) Also requests the Secretary-General to continue to assist Member States to build capacity to submit meaningful reports, and encourages States in a position to do so to provide assistance for this purpose upon request, including capacity to report on small arms and light weapons;

7. *Requests* the Secretary-General to implement the recommendations contained in his 2000, 2003, 2006, 2009 and 2013 reports on the continuing operation of the Register and its further development and to ensure that sufficient resources are made available for the Secretariat to operate and maintain the Register;

8. *Invites* the Conference on Disarmament to consider continuing its work undertaken in the field of transparency in armaments;

9. *Reiterates its call upon* all Member States to cooperate at the regional and subregional levels, taking fully into account the specific conditions prevailing in the region or subregion, with a view to enhancing and coordinating international and regional efforts aimed at increased openness and transparency in armaments;

10. *Requests* the Secretary-General to report to the General Assembly at its seventy-first session on progress made in implementing the present resolution;

11. *Decides* to include in the provisional agenda of its seventy-first session, under the item entitled "General and complete disarmament", the sub-item entitled "Transparency in armaments".

60th plenary meeting
5 December 2013

List of "Blue Book" Study Series

No.

No.	Year	Title
36	2017	The Global Reported Arms Trade
35	2015	Study on a Treaty Banning the Production of Fissile Material for Nuclear Weapons or Other Nuclear Explosive Devices
34	2013	Transparency and Confidence-Building Measures in Outer Space Activities
33	2011	Developments in the Field of Information and Telecommunications in the Context of International Security
32	2008	Verification in all its aspects, including the role of the United Nations in the field of verification
31	2005	The relationship between disarmament and development in the current international context
30	2003	Study on disarmament and non-proliferation education
29	2003	The issue of missiles in all its aspects
28	1999	Small Arms
27	1994	Study on the Application of Confidence-building Measures in Outer Space
26	1993	Study on Defensive Security Concepts and Policies
25	1993	Potential Uses of Military-Related Resources for Protection of the Environment
24	1992	Study on Ways and Means of Promoting Transparency in International Transfers of Conventional Arms
23	1991	South Africa's Nuclear-Tipped Ballistic Missile Capability
22	1991	Effective and Verifiable Measures Which Would Facilitate the Establishment of a Nuclear-weapon-free Zone in the Middle East
21	1991	Nuclear Weapons: A Comprehensive Study
20	1991	The role of the United Nations in the Field of Verification
19	1989	Study on the Economic and Social Consequences of the Arms Race and Military Expenditures
18	1989	Study on the Climatic and Other Global Effects of Nuclear War
17	1987	Study on Deterrence
16	1986	The Naval Arms Race
15	1986	Reduction of Military Budgets
14	1986	Concepts of Security
13	1985	Unilateral Nuclear Disarmament Measures
12	1985	Study on Conventional Disarmament
11	1983	Economic and Social Consequences of the Arms Race and of Military Expenditures
10	1983	Reduction of Military Budgets
9	1983	The Implications of Establishing an International Satellite Monitoring Agency
8	1982	Relationship between Disarmament and International Security
7	1982	Comprehensive Study on Confidence-building Measures
6	1982	Study on Israeli Nuclear Armament
5	1982	The Relationship between Disarmament and Development (see also No. 31, 2005)
4	1981	Reduction of Military Budgets
3	1981	Study on all the aspects of Regional Disarmament
2	1981	South Africa's plan and capability in the nuclear field
1	1981	Comprehensive Study on Nuclear Weapons (see also No. 21, 1991)